Fighting the Mafia
the
and Renewing Sicilian Culture

LEOLUCA ORLANDO

ENCOUNTER BOOKS
SAN FRANCISCO

First edition published in 2001 by Encounter Books, an activity of Encounter for
Culture and Education, Inc., a nonprofit tax exempt corporation.

Encounter Books website address: www.encounterbooks.com

Cover and text design © Ayelet Maida, A/M Studios.
Cover photograph © Shobha, Agenzia Contrasto.
Back cover photograph © Publifoto.
Photographs courtesy of the author, unless otherwise indicated.

Manufactured in the United States and printed on acid-free paper.
The paper used in this publication meets the minimum requirements of
ANSI/NISO Z39.48-1992 (R 1997) (Permanence of Paper).

Library of Congress Cataloging-in-Publication Data
Orlando, Leoluca, 1947– .
    Fighting the Mafia and renewing Sicilian culture / Leoluca Orlando.
        p. cm.
    Includes index.
    ISBN 1-893554-22-8 (cloth : alk.)
1. Orlando, Leoluca. 2. Partito della democrazia cristiana—Biography.
3. Mafia—Italy—Palermo. 4. Mayors—Italy—Palermo—Biography.
5. Palermo (Italy)—Politics and government—1945– . I. Title.

HV6453.I83 M3574 2001
364.1'06'09458—dc21   2001033338

10 9 8 7 6 5 4 3 2 1

Contents

Prologue

It was June of 1999 when Palermo finally ceased to be a Third World city—a city of which a French traveler in the previous century justly said that "even the lemon and orange blossoms smell of corpses"—and became a great European city at last.

I had been predicting this transformation all those years that Palermo was known throughout the world only as the Lebanon of Italy, a shooting gallery for the Mafia where bloody, bullet-riddled bodies littered the streets and women dressed in Sicilian black stared down at the "illustrious corpses" with looks of inexpressible grief. I knew my city well enough to know that someday we would leave this deathscape behind us and reclaim those distinctive Sicilian values—family, friendship, honor—that the Mafia had hijacked during its tenure as our national parasite and degraded into things sinister and malign. But my predictions were discounted because, after all, I was the mayor of Palermo and I had to put a good face on our hideous reality.

In the 1980s and early 1990s, the body count mounted into the thousands, including such eminent figures as the general in charge of our security forces, the chief of detectives, the chief of police, and two of the most famous magistrates in Europe. According to some estimates, there were more victims than in Palestine or Belfast or the other troubled places that monopolized the world's attention. So my critics would sometimes snidely ask, "And where is this

First World city now, this great European city we have heard so much about?"

Even in those times of criminal holocaust, I believed that Palermo would eventually choose life, because I believe that human nature is good and God is just. But while I was certain that this transformation would someday come about, I will admit that often during the last two decades—Sicily's years of living dangerously—I did not believe it would occur in my lifetime. As I walked through Palermo in the summer of 1999, however, I saw a place that was incredibly alive and, even more amazing, quite unafraid. Strolling along the side streets and boulevards, I could see the real Sicily, a land which, far from being a grim embodiment of human evil, has always been a map of human possibility.

A thousand years ago, the Moors defined Sicily as "the meeting point." Theirs was essentially a religious definition: they believed that the light of Allah, the light of Prophecy, shone with particular warmth upon them here. But in fact, many cultures met and merged on this island. If I were to say that the Sicilian is Greek, Arab, Spanish and French, in addition to being Italian, I would be speaking truth—but only a piece of it. We never really drove out the many invaders who conquered us through the millennia; we just absorbed them and turned them into Sicilians. Yet ironically, to meet our true identity, we needed finally to take up arms against the one part of us that seemed most intrinsic, but was actually most foreign of all: the Mafia and its culture of death.

I could cite statistics showing the change that resulted when we did. After all that time during which hundreds were killed every year, for instance, there were just eleven murders in Palermo in 1999, none of them Mafia-related. Yet the real proof that the long siege had finally been lifted was in the quality of life on our streets and in our public places. People congregated in the Vucciria, our traditional street market, and no longer thought twice before entering the Kalsa, the old Arab quarter—both places considered dangerous not long before. Free at last to inhabit their own city, they gathered at rediscovered monuments like Santa Maria dello Spasimo, the sixteenth-century church whose nave, never finished and open to the skies, provided moonlight theater as dramatic as the Baths of Caracalla in Rome.

Perhaps the one place that encapsulated Palermo's reemergence as a city of life was the Teatro Massimo. At the time of its opening in 1897, it was one of Europe's finest opera stages; and from the moment a young tenor named Enrico Caruso sang Ponchielli's *La Gioconda* that first season, it became an obligatory stop for the world's foremost opera singers. In 1974, this great monument was closed for "urgent, immediate repairs" which were supposed to be finished in six months, but stretched out over the next twenty-three years, as most of the many billion lire earmarked by the Italian government for the renovation disappeared—with the complicity of local officials and politicians—into the pockets of contractors linked to Mafia bosses.

The great opera voices faded into a dim echo of distant grandeur as the Teatro Massimo continued to decay. Its only function was to remind us of the fine civic life that had been stolen from us, and to provide a private parlor for a group that met daily in the basement to socialize and play cards. Nobody appeared to care that Mafiosi regularly mingled there with journalists and professionals.

Then in 1996, as if to confirm that the plague of illegality and violence was subsiding, renovation work on the Teatro Massimo was at last resumed. Within a year it was refurbished in all its glory, including the gilded frieze that reads, "Art Renews the People and Reveals Their Life." On the night of the grand reopening, the people of Palermo turned out in the thousands. They were not first-nighters, and they didn't care whether they got inside or not. It was enough simply to be present as this magnificent building was born again.

Yet in June 1999, the year Palermo served notice that it had returned to the land of the living, the Teatro Massimo was more than a symbol. It was also the site for opening ceremonies of the international conference of CIVITAS, an international organization dedicated to promoting civic education and the values of freedom.

In hosting this conference, Palermo was offering itself as an example to the delegates who came from eighty countries around the world, including places like Russia and Georgia and Rwanda and Uganda, where civil society is more imperiled than it ever was in Sicily during the darkest days of Mafia domination. The keynote for CIVITAS was given by American First Lady Hillary Clinton, who, echoing John Kennedy's famous Berlin speech, told delegates that those who doubted the ability of a citizens' movement to build democracy need only come to Palermo. She talked at length of the lessons my city offered those parts of the world that still suffered from epidemics of crime and lawlessness, emphasizing that it was the people, not the politicians, who had to decide that "enough was enough" and begin slowly taking back their city, their country and their very lives from the evil forces that had long controlled them.

As she spoke, I could see that people like Pino Arlacchi, who had fought the good fight against the Mafia as an Italian citizen and later as deputy secretary general of the United Nations, recognized what a charmed moment this was. Much-abused Palermo was once again the crossroads of the Mediterranean, as it had been in earlier centuries when Phoenicians, Carthaginians, Greeks, Romans, Moors, Normans, and finally Italians came here and left their mark. And the commerce now would not be in heroin and murder, as it had been over the last quarter-century, but in ideas about how cities and cultures are renewed.

The delegates from CIVITAS and the tens of thousands of other tourists crowding Palermo during these summer days were of course aware of our grim history. It was not hard to find vestiges of that other Palermo, the one called, as early as the 1765 edition of Diderot's *Encyclopedie*, a *ville destruite*—a city destroyed by repeated invasion during the nineteenth century; by the Allied bombardment in World War II; and most of all by the Mafia building program aptly named the "Sack of Palermo," which turned a grand city that had survived so much and still managed to remain beautiful into something ugly and haggard.

Palermo had been destroyed most of all by murder, particularly the murder of those who had tried to save the city from itself. There had been many fallen heroes over the years, the death of each one depleting Palermo a little more of its hope and will. When General Carlo Alberto Dalla Chiesa, who had become famous for subduing the Red Brigades, was gunned down in Palermo in 1982, the city's newspapers showed his bloody body, with that of his lovely young wife beside him, under the headline: "Here dies the hope of honest Palermitans." And then in 1992, hope died again when Giovanni Falcone and Paolo Borsellino, courageous magistrates who had brought the Mafia to judgment in an internationally celebrated trial, were blown up by car bombs, actions which for a few weeks seemed to mark the beginning of a coup against the government of Rome as well as Sicily, and against the very concept of human decency.

But even in our darkest hour, although we didn't know it then, a new life was stirring. One sign was in the hand-lettered placard that went up after the double martyrdom of Falcone and Borsellino: "Today begins a dawn that will see no sunset." And by the summer of 1999, the sun was shining brightly indeed.

There was the wonder of being normal—for instance, being normally curious about the doings of the First Lady and her entourage of over a hundred, who had taken over the stately Villa Igiea hotel, once the personal residence of a Sicilian family that made a vast fortune in tuna fishing at the turn of the century. And about what Chelsea Clinton was doing when she went out night-clubbing, together with my daughter Leila, in parts of the city that a few years earlier would have been off limits for any decent young woman, let alone the daughter of a president. How far we had progressed was clear when I took some CIVITAS delegates to Corleone, birthplace of the bloodthirsty sect that had destroyed the "old" Mafia in a struggle for power that claimed over a thousand victims. The streets we walked were now beginning to look like a museum of crimes past. At the town hall we had a public discussion of the Corleonesi's *mafia gangsteristica*, which had terrorized Palermo and indeed all of Sicily. A short time earlier, this would have been an act of bravado swiftly punished; but now it was simply a tour of a dead past whose criminals eventually choked on the blood they shed.

What was the lesson I drew from our recent history? the CIVITAS delegates asked. I replied that our struggle showed that the law court is only one front in the campaign against violence and lawlessness. The other is culture. An image that occurred to me early in my own fight against the Mafia was of a cart with two wheels, one law enforcement and the other culture. If one wheel turned without the other, the cart would go in circles. If both turned together, the cart would go forward.

So, at the same time as brave lawmen and prosecutors were dying in order to establish a rule of law, we were trying to rebuild our civic life: repossessing symbols like the Teatro Massimo; taking back our politics after a generation of collusion; and perhaps most important, reclaiming our children and their future. Along with our public places, the Mafia had taken over our educational system—not only because it knew that maintaining ignorance among the people was the key to its power, but also because there was money to be made. We stopped renting school space from Mafia front men and women. We began to implement an antimafia curriculum. One of the children's art pieces shown to Hillary Clinton when she toured our city depicted children holding hands around a criminal with a gun, isolated within their circle.

We also began to work with the children in the "Adopt a Monument" program. In the average American or European city, even a run-down one, such an effort would have been simply a modest attempt at social uplift. In Palermo it was a revolutionary break with the past, because the Mafia, like any totalitarian force, gets its power largely by stifling cultural memory and civic identity. In the last few years, some 25,000 students have adopted over 160 monuments in Palermo: churches with murals to be uncovered; public offices of earlier centuries to be painted and brought back into service; parks to be made green and blooming again. As they demanded that the dirt be removed from these monuments, our children knew their work was a metaphor for cleansing the spiritual grime deposited by years of criminal rule.

I told the delegates of CIVITAS that the chief lesson of the Palermo renaissance was that while it is possible to lose momentum or even slip backward in the political/legal realm—as evident in the moral stammering that has defined the Italian government's response to the Mafia—there is no backtracking in the civic realm. People who have known freedom will not willingly go back to degraded collective lives. They will not unsay words like "Mafia" once they have been said. They will not become stupid about democracy once they have experienced it. They will not again surrender the monuments and public places that show where they came from and define who they are.

As Paolo Borsellino, the courageous magistrate and my old friend who died for this new Palermo, once said, "The solution to the problem of the Mafia is to make the state work." This is partly a matter of justice and the rule of law. It is also a question of meeting human needs in the civic realm, from the need for jobs that don't involve collusion with a criminal conspiracy, to the need for democracy and a culture of freedom.

| | |

During the summer of 1999, when I looked at my city as if with new eyes, I also looked at myself and, as I often have over the past few years, felt amazed to be alive. For many years—a longer time than I care to remember—I was a marked man. The question was not whether I would be killed, but when and how. In a special it did on me, England's Channel Four called me "the Walking Corpse." And that is how I felt. I experienced death vicariously every day. But then, as the people of Palermo began to enter their new dawn, I had a sudden thought: "Good Lord, I might actually live!" How would I spend this extra life I had been granted? The answer was easy: making this city great again.

I still have a dozen bodyguards, and we all move in armored

cars. I still instinctively duck when I hear a backfire and look nervously over my shoulder. I know that the Mafia is still out there, haunting the Sicilian sleep. Yet although the stake has not yet been driven through its heart, the organization is dead. It died the minute it was expelled from the political system where it had come to dwell during its long sojourn in our national life. The Mafia no longer rules us. It is outside our local government now. Palermo is no longer a pariah among cities. When Moody International Certification recently gave us one of its highest issuer ratings, Aa3, the same as Stockholm and Barcelona and higher than New York, it thereby announced that the changes in Palermo over the previous few years were structural and profound, fully warranting that sign of confidence.

For a city that has lived in the shadows to come out into the sunlight again is a miracle. Yet this miracle has not been without cost, and I often pause at some moment during my day to think of all those who died—the brave and the ordinary; the major characters, the supporting actors, and the bystanders. I want to believe that their deaths have not been in vain, and sometimes do. For I believe that what has occurred in Sicily is in fact an epic story, a story of death *and* transfiguration. Walking through Palermo in the summer of 1999 and afterward, I have often felt a survivor's special guilt, and also a survivor's unique responsibility: to tell the story as it happened.

After long treating the concept as taboo, linguists now speculate endlessly about the origins of the word "Mafia." Some say it comes from *Mahias*, Arabic for "bold" or "braggart." Others say that its root is *Muafirr*, the name of a Saracen tribe that once controlled Palermo. Less plausibly, it has been suggested that the word comes from *M'fie*, the name of the caves that served as hiding places for those Saracens and later for Sicilians who retreated there in fear when Garibaldi landed in 1861.

The theory that has always seemed most reasonable to me holds that "Mafia" is a corruption of the Arabic *Mu* ("strength") plus *Afah* ("to protect"). Yet what I find most intriguing about this word is not the exotic etymologies reaching far back into Sicilian history, but the fact that during the years of my youth, "Mafia" was almost never said. I was aware that it existed—both the word and the reality it stood for—but I apprehended it the same way that one catches a faint aroma on the wind, something familiar yet not quite identifiable.

The spectral presence of the Mafia in Sicilian life has always made me think of the comment by the Danish philosopher Sören Kierkegaard that part of our human dilemma is to be condemned to live our lives forward and understand them backward. We Sicilians have lived for generations with the Mafia, while rigorously excluding it not only from our conversation but even from our thought. Only relatively recently have we begun to understand backward the impact that "the Octopus"—a metaphor for Cosa Nostra first used by a judge and soon after a common term—has had on our history and culture.

Yet Sicily is the logical place for a phenomenon such as the Mafia to have arisen. We are a people who never really ruled our own territory. We were always a colony, and, even worse, a colony passed from one ruler to another. If these rulers had been harsh and repressive, they would at least have created a strong centralized government; but this was not the case. Sicily was always a place to be exploited more than governed. Until the nineteenth century, aristocratic families controlled Sicilian life more or less independently of whatever conqueror happened to be ruling at any given time. These barons cared about their own property and prerogatives, but not much else. Their ethos is beautifully portrayed in Giuseppe di Lampedusa's *The Leopard*, where Fabrizio, the Prince, sleepwalks through life, disconnected from his country, his fate, and even his own ancestral holdings.

Eventually this aristocracy would collapse and disappear, but without leaving a middle class to fill the vacuum it left behind. Instead, as the barons moved to Rome, Vienna, Paris and other more cosmopolitan areas, the administration of their lands fell to middlemen called *gabelloti*. These administrators squeezed the sharecroppers to pay the high rents demanded by absentee landowners, and controlled the brigands who roamed the countryside. Backed by a network of family, friends, and clients—the only groups able to provide social stability in the absence of an institutional order— these *gabelloti* became Sicily's New Men, archetypes of the *capimafia* of the future. (Lampedusa's Don Cologero is such a man *avant la lettre*.) The violent men they hired to enforce their power would become the Mafiosi of Sicily's future.

Unlike its equivalent in the United States, which was based on family (Gambino, Bonanno and the like), the Sicilian Mafia was rooted in the land and organized around a place—Corleone, Prizzi, and other communities. Eventually the Mafia groupings in these places would build a bridge from the village to the developing urban centers such as Palermo. The Sicilian Cosa Nostra was always more intrinsic to the structure of society than its American cousins. It developed because the state itself was atrophied and defective in Sicily, and the people, conquered repeatedly by outsiders, never expected to receive justice from "the system." They looked to the charismatic *uomini di rispetto* to fulfill the functions that bureaucratic governments served everywhere else in Europe. If your daughter was raped, you looked to such a "man of respect" for redress rather than to a distant and foreign police force.

The Mafia networks of the nineteenth century gradually took on the functions of the state: collecting taxes, providing a hierarchy of leadership, and raising little armies to enforce its "laws." Political and economic life adjusted to these arrangements and accepted them as reality. Later on, when legitimate government tried to assert its authority, it would first have to redefine this reality as "criminal." This was a monumental task. It is the subject of this book.

The Mafia created an autonomous social order in Sicily, but it could not have succeeded as well as it did, had it not also created a myth: that its members were Men of Honor comprising an honorable society that not only made the social order work, but made it work according to principle. Mario Puzo, author of *The Godfather*, got this aspect of the Mafia mentality exactly right: those who chose this path believed that while they might be called upon to perform tasks others might shrink from in serving their family and friends, they were nonetheless superior to the corrupt and hypocritical world surrounding them.

| | |

A sign of how deeply—and swiftly—the Mafia had penetrated Sicilian life came in 1893 when a man named Emanuele Notarbartolo, director general of the Bank of Sicily and former mayor of Palermo, tried to overturn corrupt deals made by one of his directors, a politician named Raffaele Palizzolo, who had links to the Mafia. Notarbartolo bravely protested these criminal activities to ministers in Rome. Before the issue could be brought to trial, he was stabbed twenty-six times by an assassin on a train, becoming the first of many "excellent cadavers" in Sicily's future.

The entrenchment of the Mafia, complete by the 1920s, made this organization a public enemy for Mussolini. Upon coming to power, the Fascists saw the Mafia for what it was even then: *una associazione per delinquere*, in the words of Cesare Mori, "an association for criminal purposes." Mori, who became known as the "Iron Prefect" after Mussolini sent him to Sicily to bring the Mafia to heel, famously swept into the centers of Mafia power and bluntly laid out his intentions to the townspeople: "My name is Mori and I shall have people killed. Delinquency must disappear just as the dust disappears on the wind of the sirocco."

A measure of the cleansing power of his sirocco could be seen in the fact that in 1928, the year that Mori took control, there were only 26 murders in Sicily compared to 278 the year before. But most of the "men of honor" he rounded up, killed, imprisoned or sentenced to hard labor were at the level of the *picciotti*, or soldiers. The bosses went into hiding or slipped away to the United States, Marseilles, or even Tunis, pretending to be heroic figures of resistance. And when, in 1929, Mori began to investigate the connections between the Mafia and some high-level figures of the Fascist regime, a telegram from Rome informed him that he had been pensioned off. He was thus the first to understand what others would see later on: it was far easier to deal with the Mafia militarily than to root the organization out of Sicilian politics and culture.

After the Allied invasion of 1943, the Fascists fled to the mainland as the Allies advanced on Palermo. American soldiers saw chaos: criminals escaping from jails, peasants occupying land, people settling private feuds with murder and arson, and everyone stealing anything that could be carried. General George Patton said of the Palermitans: "These people are crazy!" Such a view made any structure of influence appealing. While it is a myth that the

Allies used American mobsters like "Lucky" Luciano to inspire an anti-Fascist Mafia underground in Sicily, it is true that some Americans naively failed to exclude the Mafia from the postwar social order. In fact, in one letter to the secretary of state, the American consul wrote: "I have the honor to report that on November 18, 1944, General Giuseppe Castallaro, together with Maffia leaders including Calogero Vizzini, conferred with Virgilio Nasi, head of the well known Nasi family of Trapani and asked him to take part in the leadership of a Maffia-backed movement for Sicilian autonomy."

The United States dropped the idea of Sicilian separatism once the Germans were driven out of Italy, but didn't shed its naiveté about the Mafia. After 1945, with the long-delayed issues of land redistribution and union organizing finally coming to the fore in Sicily, a force that could counterbalance the Left was vitally important. Thus the Mafia was not only tolerated, but eased into an alliance with the Christian Democratic Party, which would fight the Communists in the political arena, collecting Mafia votes and sometimes using the Mafia as its military wing. This devil's pact—which resulted in the murder of dozens of Communists and Socialists over the next few years and in the delivery of votes that kept the Christian Democrats in power in Italy—would haunt Sicily for a generation.

| | |

At the time of my birth, August 1, 1947, these facts of the Mafia were not known, let alone written; the time for looking backward at its history had not yet arrived in Sicily. My parents were uneasy as they watched the Mafia use the crises of the postwar world as a cover to enter our country's political and cultural bloodstream. Yet they had more immediate concerns, notably their fear that the pneumonia which had killed their firstborn son, Carmelo, a few days after his birth in 1941 would now take me, too.

Penicillin was still an exotic substance in Sicily at the time of my infancy. But through my mother's family connections and my father's prestige as the most prominent civil lawyer in Sicily, they managed to get the precious medicine—in this case from the Vatican pharmacy—and I recovered. Yet instead of diminishing, their fears about my health became an obsession that burst into near-hysteria a few years later when it was discovered during a routine physical exam that my heart was on the wrong side of my chest. This discovery was made by a radiologist who, upon seeing an x-ray, first furiously berated his assistant for having printed the film incorrectly, only to realize after further examination that not only was the image accurate, but *all* of my organs were reversed. Since then I have always worn a gold medallion around my neck inscribed with the Latin words *Situs viscerum inversus*—and I'm sure some would say that I have pursued my political life in reverse order, too.

I had two older sisters, but I was given my dead brother's role of firstborn son, a treasured position in a Sicilian family that requires a loving diminutive, however old the boy is. I was "Luchetto," especially when my parents were exhorting me to do those things they hoped would ensure my survival. "Luchetto, put your coat on, otherwise you'll catch cold and be seriously ill!" or "Luchetto, be careful, you'll hurt yourself!" or "Luchetto, don't do that, remember that you're very fragile!" In time I would have two younger brothers and two more sisters, but in some peculiar way I would always be the baby of the family as well as the "firstborn."

Not surprisingly, I grew up with the conviction that death was anxious to claim me, and that I therefore had to live as well as I could in the brief time I had been allotted. It is probably also why later on, during the years when the Mafia had decided to kill me, I found myself not particularly afraid; after all, I had been condemned since birth. I feared the pain, but death itself had been my companion for years.

The rhythms of a Sicily that was almost gone when I was a boy and has now vanished forever were still part of my growing up. The first twenty days of our summer holidays, for instance, were always spent at Imbriaca, one of several vast agricultural properties belonging to my father in an area near Corleone, about forty miles from Palermo. Named after the Sicilian word for "drunk," Imbriaca bordered on one of the many properties owned by my mother's family. It was called Margi, which derives from the word "soaked." This area, with its breathtakingly beautiful valleys, woods and towering cliffs, has little rainfall but is very rich in underground waters, and thus all the aqueous names.

The properties of Imbriaca and Margi are separated by a stream, crossed by a small bridge which we children jokingly called the *Ponte dei Sospiri*, "the Bridge of Sighs," a reference to the romantic landmark all lovers visiting Venice feel obliged to pass under in a gondola. This bridge at Imbriaca was where my father, Salvatore Orlando, would meet my mother, Eleonora, youngest daughter of the aristocratic Cammarata family and many years his junior, when they were courting; so we imagined the romance of their trysts.

Theirs was a love match but also, by Sicilian standards, something of a mismatch as well. The Orlandos were landed gentry, and my father, whose family came from the charming town of Prizzi (in whose central square the wedding scene in *The Godfather Part II*, which supposedly takes place in Corleone, was actually shot), became a civil lawyer, just as his own father and grandfather had been. The Orlandos were part of that Catholic rural bourgeoisie whose strong moral principles became even more rigid in my father's case through study of the law in Heidelberg. His morality was matched only by his piety. My father always paid his taxes fully and punctually, while others in his social class scornfully evaded them. He was seen as foolish for complying with the letter of the law, but for him the letter was the law in microcosm.

My mother descends on one side from the Marquises of Arezzo—of the oldest mid-Italian aristocracy—and on the other from the Cammaratas, Barons of Corleone. In fact, the Cammarata family palazzo in Corleone, which dominates the small central square of the town, is now the seat of municipal government. The Sicilian heritage of the Arezzos was literary in origin, beginning when one of them wrote a biography of Charles V, Holy Roman

Emperor and King of Spain, Naples and Sicily. Charles was so pleased with this work that he showered money, titles and Sicilian land on the writer, and so the Arezzos joined the country's nobility.

The fact that my mother had technically married beneath her class sometimes worked its way into her conversation. It was her only strength against my formidable father, and she used it with elegance and innuendo, often in the form of a melancholy observation that for reasons not entirely clear to her, she did not frequent as often as before the high society salons of Palermo where she belonged by birth. In truth, it was because of my father's moral rigor, not the stigma of his bourgeois background, that both had chosen to shun this environment. Apart from close family members, I cannot recall a single friend of my mother's or father's frequently visiting our home. We were far more likely to entertain a worker or foreman from one of our country estates than non-family members of Palermo's high society.

All this struck me as quite odd when I was growing up. Eventually I realized that it was my father's way of keeping us from possibly being tainted by people casually associated (as so many upper-class Sicilians have been) with the Mafia. Later on, after the war against the Mafia had been fought and won, one of the wealthiest and best-bred individuals in Palermo, a man who had not offered any help when the fight was taking place, came up to me and said, "I want to thank you for what you've done. We offered them our fingers and they took our hands. You've given us our hands—our freedom—back again."

| | |

There was no running water in our country house at Imbriaca, and as a five-year-old my great joy was to sit astride a mule led by one of the peasants who worked for our family, and go to fetch water from the spring. The water was put into enormous clay jars, attached to stout hooks on either side of the mule's saddle, and brought back to the house, where it remained sweet and ice cold. Imbriaca had no electricity; illumination came from oil lamps, giving a dim, romantic light to our quiet evenings together. It was not until the 1960s that my father finally had a generator installed, but it made such an unholy racket at night that we switched it off and continued to go to bed with our oil lamps.

After the mule came a small Sardinian donkey. It was a present from my father and belonged to me alone. It took the place of horses, which I was rarely allowed to ride because, as the movie *Gone with the Wind* showed, they can cause one to fall and die. My parents continued to fret about their precious Luchetto's mortality, even though in fact I was as healthy as my brothers and sisters. At the slightest sign of illness, Doctor Michele Navarra—referred to as my pediatrician, although he was actually the only available doctor in Corleone—was immediately summoned to thump my chest and give them reassurances.

The word "Mafia" being forbidden in our house, it was not until several years later that I learned that Dr. Navarra, who had a leasehold on some of my mother's Cammarata family property, was also the *capomafia* of Corleone. This was at a time when drugs had not yet changed the nature of the Mafia, drowning it in money and gratuitous violence, and it was still worth a man of honor's time to administer the estate of an old aristocratic family. Some years later, Dr. Navarra's star in the Corleonese Mafia's firmament began to wane, while that of a particularly vicious criminal named Luciano Leggio was on the rise. Leggio was a cattle thief who gained control of a fleet of trucks after the Allied occupation. He used the trucks to transport the cattle he stole and slaughtered in Corleone to Palermo for sale on the black market. As Leggio's ambition grew, he ran afoul of Dr. Navarra, who lured him to a meeting with the intention of killing him. But Leggio escaped and later ambushed my old pediatrician with submachine guns as he was crossing our family estate in his car.

| | |

If Imbriaca was our retreat, the place where we lived according to the rhythms that had guided Sicilian life for generations, our regular home was a large building on Via Villafranca in the center of Palermo. Our family had the entire third floor. Below us lived two maiden sisters of my father's; and below them, another aunt with her husband and their five children. With the seven of us, that made twelve children between the two families, meaning plenty of playmates without the need to import strangers. We first measured our intelligence, power and daring in the Sicilian way: against blood relatives. Our world was complete—and completely removed from the reality of the city and the vast majority of its inhabitants.

Our home was beautiful; my mother wouldn't have allowed anything else. It was serene and full of love. But not necessarily joy. It was difficult to be joyful with our German governess, naturally called Fräulein, who was always present and ready to remind us of the rules and regulations that defined our lives. Fräulein was an elderly, tall, angular woman who uncannily embodied all of my father's rigorous principles, and perhaps for this reason clashed regularly with my mother. She was not prone to smiles, let alone jokes. But while I frequently thought of the things I would like to do to her as punishment for her tyranny, neither I nor any of my brothers and sisters dared to begin an insurrection. An assault on established order was unthinkable. Instead, we vented our frustration on each other, regularly bickering and fighting. We accepted Fräulein's right to discipline each of us individually, but never to regulate conflicts among ourselves. We were *family*, and no matter how much we fought, no one who didn't share our blood had any right to step between us.

In any case, the only punishment we truly dreaded was my father's pointed silence. Father was a large, imposing, self-contained man. But it was his eyes rather than his physical presence that cowed us. His look of disapproval was scorching when he entered the room and found us squabbling. We would all immediately fall silent. Possessing the moral equivalent of x-ray vision, his eyes would indicate who, in his opinion, was in the wrong. Without ever really being reproached, the one subjected to that withering gaze would run to his room, throw himself on his bed and cry. The next step in this ritual was for a brother or sister to quickly follow and offer consolation. The advice was always the same: "Go and apologize."

The last words of this stylized drama of guilt and repentance were always the same: "Papa, I was wrong. I beg your pardon." Whereupon my father's look immediately became tranquil and soothing. The troublemaker was given a kiss and life returned to normal once again.

At my father's insistence, our meals were the perfect expression of our way of life. Punctually at 1:30 P.M. each day we sat down for lunch, and again at exactly 8:30 for dinner—my father at the head of the table, my mother at the foot and we children arrayed always in the same configuration on either side. Our waiter/chauffeur Nino (or Vittorio Emanuele or Giuseppe, as the years passed), wearing white gloves, would serve first my mother, then my father, then each of the children. The meal was always the same: pasta, a main course and fruit. Tasty, plentiful, wholesome food; no appetizer and no dessert, both of which were considered weaknesses. No one was allowed to leave anything on the plate. That would be wasteful, and wastefulness, although we had plenty, was a sin.

Not going to Mass on Sunday was also a sin. Even more, it was simply inconceivable. We all trooped off to the local parish church every Sunday except at Christmas. This one time each year, the aristocratic side of the family was allowed to express itself and we attended midnight Mass at the Church of the Knights of Malta or the Church of the Holy Sepulcher. My father was himself a Knight of the Holy Sepulcher, a lay religious organization dating back to medieval times with its own age-old rituals, dress and traditions. After midnight Mass on Christmas Eve, we went to a reception in the Palazzo of the Princes of San Vincenzo, the same palazzo where the great Italian director Luchino Visconti filmed the famous ball scene of his film version of *The Leopard* with Burt Lancaster and

Claudia Cardinale. As I realized later when I first read this great novel, we were living in the afterglow of the world Lampedusa had portrayed.

With religion came many of the traditions that, because they were Sicilian, involved food. I remember the *panelle*, thin flat triangles made with a paste of chickpea flour and fried in sizzling oil; and the *cuccìa*, a sweet made with grain, ricotta cheese, sugar and candied fruits. Delicious! These dishes always appeared on the table on December 13, the Feast of St. Lucia, when nothing made with wheat can be eaten—no bread, no pasta, no cake containing wheat flour—because tradition tells the tale that in a terrible year of famine, when all the wheat crop had failed, a boatload of grain arrived in Palermo harbor on the Feast of St. Lucia and such was the hunger of the poor citizens that they boiled it whole and ate it without waiting to grind it into flour. Thus the legend that St. Lucia had intervened miraculously to save Palermo. Today this tradition is still respected and the Palermitans have developed various succulent dishes for this holiday, none of them containing wheat.

| | |

One day in June of 1953, my father came home after supervising the harvest at Imbriaca. Giving me a significant look, he said to my mother: "It's a disgrace that Luca is still not going to school. I've learned that the son of one of our workers went to school when he was five, and here is Luca, almost six and not yet at school." The fact that my diminutive had gone from Luchetto to Luca was significant: I was growing up. On that day more than ever before, I felt the weight of my father's expectations settling down on me.

That summer at our seaside villa in Sferracavallo ("horseshoe" in English, a reference to the shape of the small bay where the town was situated), Miss Serio, an elementary school teacher from Palermo, came every day to give me lessons. While my brothers and sisters continued to pick blackberries and ride the Sardinian donkey, I prepared to enter the world. At the end of that long, exhausting summer, I took examinations, passed, and was admitted directly into the second grade of primary school—thus, to my father's deep satisfaction, equaling the achievement of the son of one of our farm workers.

My school was Gonzaga, *the* private school of Palermo. It stood in a huge park and was run by Jesuit priests who had created a reputation for excellent academics and exacting standards of personal discipline. It was exclusively for boys (my sisters went to a private convent school), and even more exclusively, for the boys of rich families. But not the newly rich—only the rich with a name and a history. No sons of the parvenus were admitted to Gonzaga. Our morning trip to school was a stately progress in the company of Fräulein and the chauffeur who commanded the large black Mercedes. First my sisters were dropped off at the Sacred Heart, and then we three boys were taken to Gonzaga where our day began with Mass in the small chapel.

I remember two things from those days: sore knees from kneeling, and the black smock with a starched collar we were forced to wear. I hated that smock! In the garden there was a fountain with several taps, and during recess I often "accidentally" got my smock soaked so I would have an excuse for not putting it back on over my shorts when we returned to class. For years my ultimate ambition was to lose the smock and gain long trousers. In the meantime I had a proximate ambition: to become a member of the choir. This was not because I had any particular love of music or could sing very well. In fact, I was tone-deaf. But the choir members wore a *special* smock that was slightly more tolerable than the regular one. Finally, moved by my pathetic persistence, my teachers agreed to put me in the choir on one condition: I was to move my mouth but, on pain of immediate expulsion, I was *not* to sing. Not one note.

My satisfaction was enormous. The special smock allowed me to feel that I had *bella figura*. This concept, which might be understood as "cutting an impressive figure," is of course almost a secular religion to all Italians, but especially to Sicilians, for whom the elegant appearance has traditionally masked and to some degree transformed the impoverished reality. I have more than once asked a friend, after giving a speech, how it went, and received what I must admit was a satisfying response: "Luca, you talked a load of nonsense, but you had *bella figura*."

Returning home after choir practice in my special smock, I found no deep appreciation for music there, either. It's true that my father would frequently sing a few lines of some aria to help him underline a point he was trying to make, and attending the opera in our family box at the Teatro Massimo was another ritual in our lives. But while we never missed an opening night, I am sad to say that music was not part of our soul. It was an elegant dress one wore on certain occasions and part of the language of our social class, a language whose most important phrase, it sometimes seemed, was *bella figura*.

| | |

The rebellious spirit I repressed at home exploded at Gonzaga. During my first six years there, I was always at the bottom of the class. I refused to study and chose friends who had the same attitude. The result was that at the end of each academic year I had to endure a conference with my parents in which they were told, "This year we'll promote him…" There was another clause not spoken though strongly implied: "but probably not next year." And indeed, year by year more of my friends dropped behind. Then, at the age of eleven, I found myself alone. The last of my obstinate friends, Attilio, had failed because an exasperated teacher had discovered that he could barely read. So I spent that year at the bottom of the class by myself.

The next fall, though, something clicked. It was as if I said to myself, "Enough!" Expending not much more effort to succeed than I had at failing, I soon reached the top of my class and stayed there. The fact that one could completely change the course of his life was a lesson that had a continuing impact on me. If an individual could say "Enough," it occurred to me later on, why not a group? If a group, why not a neighborhood? If a neighborhood, why not a city?

I was now a good student, but still had trouble behaving. To be promoted each year, one had to receive a grade of 8 in *condotta*. I was lucky to get a 7, which meant a continuation of the year-end negotiations between my parents and school officials.

One teacher I had particular difficulty getting along with was Father Barbosio, who taught science. I regarded many of the things he said as both scientifically and morally questionable, and arrogantly went out of my way to ridicule him. I also played infantile pranks on him. In the middle of an experiment, for instance, I would sneak to the power switch and turn it off, rendering all the work done up until then useless. During a test, I would pass my own invariably excellent notes to other students—in particular to those who hadn't studied.

After putting up with such behavior longer than he should have, Father Barbosio finally took me aside: "Look, it's useless continuing this way. You misbehave, I have to throw you out, and you stand in the hall the rest of the hour. Let's save time. The moment I enter the classroom, you exit."

So for two years I passed every science hour out in the corridor, forced to stand up straight near the door with folded arms— no lounging, no leaning against the wall. Father Barbosio questioned the other students about the content of past lessons in strict alphabetical order, which gave them a sense of when they'd be called on. But not me. At any time I could be asked to step in from the hall and answer a question. A perhaps unintended consequence of this arrangement was that I was the only one in the class who thoroughly studied everything.

I made trouble in large part because I was confused about practically everything, although I thought I had everything well under control. This arrogance was shaken in high school when I heard there were one or two boys who knew about or had had sex. We used the phrase "having sex" with braggadocio, but for me at least, the reality behind it was a mystery. I had grown up believing firmly in the equation that is central to a certain kind of Catholicism: body + sex = sin. Everything that had to do with the body, in fact, was not only sinful but stupid. I remember once during our infrequent gym exercises we were climbing a rope. I was barely able to clear the floor, and felt quite virtuous about it. "Look at him!" I remember thinking about a classmate who nimbly shinnied up the rope, "He's really stupid!"

It was little wonder that I drove all of the teachers and administrators crazy. As I look back on this, I am not particularly proud. There was nothing funny in my behavior. Yet I cannot help but smile at the memory of the dean, whom I had one day driven entirely out of his wits, chasing me down the corridor in an effort to place a (probably well-deserved) kick on my backside. I swerved to escape the kick and his shoe flew off and landed on the head of an innocent student, an open-mouthed spectator to this extraordinary scene.

| | |

In another country at another time, perhaps, school would have been the transitional stage out into civic life. But not in Sicily in the 1950s. It was still inside the family where most of the social lessons were learned. I have a vivid memory, for instance, of an afternoon during the period when I was having such behavior problems in school, when my father was late for lunch. This in itself was unheard of. We children peered through the shutters—closed to keep out the heat—on the lookout for the arrival of his car. We never would have considered eating without him. We couldn't have, even if we wanted to: Giuseppe was with him, and for us to eat, he would have to remove his chauffeur's hat and jacket, then put on his white jacket and white gloves and serve at the table.

My mother told us that Papa was seeing Cardinal Ruffini, archbishop of Palermo, a figure I thought of as being only one small step down from the Pope, who was himself but one step down from

God. But this did not make the waiting any easier. Finally, at two o'clock, the car turned into the driveway.

Papa came in and brusquely apologized for his lateness, and then we sat down.

"Have you been with His Eminence?" my mother asked after we had been eating in silence for several minutes.

"Yes." My father did not look up.

"You're quite late," she prodded a minute or so later.

"Yes. A long conversation."

As we continued eating, it suddenly seemed as if my parents were alone together in a room where the rest of us could watch but not enter. This was a room filled with looks and strategic pauses more than words.

"What did you talk about?"

"You know, Pina,"—my father's rare use of my mother's nickname heightened the sense of a privileged communication between them—"His Eminence asked me to stand as candidate for the Christian Democrats at the next elections. He assured me that I would have the full support of the Church."

"And?" my mother prompted.

"And I refused."

Why? My mother didn't ask the question. I did—silently and without even looking up. *Why didn't you become a candidate?* My father could have become a member of Parliament and he refused! He could have been in Rome with ministers and heads of state and he refused!

My father spoke again, almost as if responding to me directly: "If I were to stand for the Christian Democrats, I would have to accept votes from the Mafia."

He had finally said the word! My mind was whirling. I felt almost drunk from this unexpected cocktail comprised of these strong ingredients: the cardinal, the Christian Democrats, the Mafia and my father. What had the cardinal to do with the Mafia? What were Mafia votes, and why would Papa have to accept them if he stood for the Christian Democrats? The pieces might have fallen into place if I had known that at about this time, Cardinal Ruffini had gotten a letter of inquiry from the Vatican in response to the charge of a courageous Protestant clergyman that Sicily was controlled by the Mafia. Ruffini had responded with what had been his position—and that of the local church—for decades: Sicilians are decent, hard-working people libeled by such an accusation. There is no such thing as an organization called the Mafia; there are only individual criminals.

The private intellectual room my parents shared was suffused with that suffocating mutual understanding I had sensed on other occasions—when, for instance, we were all ready to depart for the country, our cases packed in the black Mercedes, and suddenly we would be told, "We're not going now." We couldn't leave, not even traveling as we were accustomed to do: always by daylight, and whenever possible in convoy with other family members in several cars, the adults alert and cautious. This was considered not so much taking precautions, as simply the way we moved, part of our manner of life. Only many years later did I learn that there had been a constant danger of kidnapping. Eventually it stopped, not because the Mafia had a change of heart toward the inhabitants of their own land, but simply because this was a crime that brought too many *carabinieri* to scour the countryside, thus hampering other, more lucrative criminal activities.

I had the same feeling—that there was something out there I wasn't quite getting—when my father would come home and say something like this to my mother: "I saw Cavaliere Peppino. He greeted me and I answered him politely. Fortunately he didn't ask to come here to our home." Or when I saw his reaction to certain distant cousins who had allied themselves by marriage to families whose surnames would be mentioned with a particular look or tone of voice. Such matters were so freighted with taboo that we children didn't even ask each other—and even less thought of asking our parents—"What is this all about?" Certain things were just the way they were. If we were no longer leaving for the country, obviously there was a reason. If some people, even relatives, were not to be associated with, obviously there was a reason. But we didn't speak of it.

So the feeling was familiar, yet this memorable lunch was somewhat different. It was when the idea of the Mafia as a reality, not just a word, began to inhabit my mind. It was not only evil, but ambiguous, perverse, contaminating. It stained those who were touched by it and even those who weren't.

Later on, when I was engaged in my fight against the Mafia, rumors circulated that my father, morally the most impeccable man I have ever known, had himself been a Mafia *consigliore*. (The *consigliore* is an advisor who is outside the organization, unlike the *consigliere*, the lawyer/advisor who is inside the family.) He was guilty by syllogism: he was a man of power; Mafia men are powerful; therefore he must be connected to the Mafia. When I sued the author of this slander and got a final judgment for 100 million lire, these rumors immediately stopped.

| | |

The subject of the Mafia was never, in all my school years, mentioned at Gonzaga, not even in high school. Not that the subject was avoided; it simply didn't exist. We all lived under a bell jar— not only the children of wealthy families attending Gonzaga, but all Sicilians. Our ignorance was willful; today it would be called "denial." The Mafia might well be virtually invisible as an organization, yet it could be seen in its works, not just in the occasional death, but also in the changing face of our city. For it was in the 1950s and '60s that what later became known as the "Sack of Palermo" was taking place.

After the war, there had finally been land reform. The effect, paradoxically, was not so much that a few peasants got a few acres of their own, but that many others were freed from the land altogether. Hundreds of thousands left farms for the city. Their arrival touched off a postwar building boom. In Sicily some 70 percent of the GNP is government, and government is always building, always spending money. But this building boom was unlike any other.

It coincided with the rise of two young men, Salvo Lima and Vito Ciancimino. Lima had Mafia in his blood: he was the son of a Mafioso named Vincenzo Lima. Ciancimino was a "made" member of Cosa Nostra. The two men moved into the leadership of Palermo's Christian Democrats in the 1950s, the first generation of politicians with clear Mafia ties. By the early 1960s Lima was mayor of Palermo and Ciancimino was his commissioner for public works—by far the most important of all the departments. Together they supervised the design of the city's infamous "Town Plan," which became, in effect, the manifesto for the Sack of Palermo.

Development was forced into green areas on the outskirts of the city, areas invariably owned by "friends of the friends," which immediately skyrocketed in value. A style of architecture that can only be called Mafia Modern sprang up there: boxy cement dormitories for the immigrants from rural areas, shoddy structures of indignity packed with poor people who received no municipal services once they were settled there. (Some areas in the city received no deliveries of water, gas, and electricity not just for days or even months, but for years!) Looking at these concrete jungles, one could understand why Sicilians were the largest per capita consumers on earth not only of olive oil, tomatoes, and anchovies, but also of cement.

Lima and Ciancimino oversaw the blueprint for the Sack, and allowed the Mafia to supervise it through construction-business fronts that made astronomical profits. Their construction was actually destruction in disguise. The wonderful Conca d'Oro (Golden Vale), once full of orange groves whose blossoms perfumed the air in springtime, was eaten up by cement. And the same fate overtook other areas like Piana dei Colli, famed for its magnificent seventeenth- and eighteenth-century villas.

My father managed to save our home by convincing the authorities to designate it as historically important. (This allowed him to tell those who approached him to buy and tear down and ultimately replace the building that unfortunately his hands were tied.) But many wealthy homeowners did not take these steps. In fact they collaborated with the construction Mafia. Beautiful art nouveau villas along the Via Libertà were destroyed to make room for apartments. Many of the structures protected by their landmark status were allowed to decay, the owners hoping that if they eventually became dangerous enough, demolition would finally be allowed.

The result was the destruction of a city and its spirit. In addition to the concrete warrens on the outskirts of town, there were surreal projects like roads leading to dead ends and factories that never produced anything, while the center of the city was left to implode from neglect. Magnificent Moorish buildings and Norman churches deteriorated amidst a bombed-out decay similar to that of New York's Bedford-Stuyvesant. The population of the city center decreased from over a hundred thousand to less than forty thousand almost overnight, with those left living in Third World squalor.

And while all this happened—the remaking of Palermo into a Mafiapolis—nobody said a word. The Mafia code of *omertà*, silence, had long since become a national affliction.

2

In 1965 I took my final high school exam. Called the *Maturità*, it is administered by a public commission and focuses on an area of academic specialization, mine being Greek and Latin. The most prestigious public school in Palermo was the Garibaldi, and there was a lively competition between its pupils, known as the *Garibaldini*, and the *Gonzaghini*, as we were called. On our part the rivalry was tinged with envy, not only because the Garibaldi was a co-ed school but also because it had as good an academic record as Gonzaga, but without the repressive atmosphere that characterized our school.

That year I had the highest marks of any *Maturità classica* in Italy. I became something of a phenomenon and ended up in all the Sicilian newspapers. In a sudden accession of pride and enthusiasm, my father ordered a magnificent car for me, a red Porsche. But after getting some perspective on my achievement, he decided that it would not be "educational" for an eighteen-year-old to have such a flashy and expensive vehicle, and he bought me a small Fiat instead. Since I had never even been allowed to own a moped, I was thrilled to have any car at all.

As it turned out, the local Communist afternoon newspaper, *L'Ora*, had staged a competition in which the student in the province of Palermo scoring highest on the *Maturità classica* would win ten days in Moscow, all expenses paid. So as soon as the results of the exam were made public, I went to *L'Ora*'s headquarters to claim my prize. After a long wait, I was finally received by one of the editors. As I explained who I was, he got the look on his face of someone suddenly forced to converse with an extraterrestrial. It was 1965, a high point in the Cold War, and here was a *Gonzaghino* produced by the Jesuits, sworn enemies of the Communists, trying to collect a free trip to the motherland!

"You can't participate," he said.

"Why not?"

"Because you come from a private school."

"Whether I studied at a private school or studied in Timbuktu has nothing to do with it. I sat for the exams in front of a public commission, just like everybody else! You promised a trip for the highest score. I got it."

A look combining boredom and triumph came over his face: "I'm sorry, but we can't permit a pupil from a private school—and a religious one at that—to go to Moscow."

The trip went to Salvino Mazzamuto, the boy whose score was just below mine. He had attended a public school and was an activist in the young Communist movement, and he would later become a good friend of mine.

This episode had an odd effect on me. At first I felt a keen sense of injustice. But then, as that emotion receded, I began to wonder if the contempt I had seen in the eyes of the editor of *L'Ora* might somehow be justified. It was true that my social world thus far had been bounded by the walls of my family's palazzo in Palermo and our villas in the country and at the seaside, and by the walls holding in my companions and me at Gonzaga—all of us rich, Catholic Daddy's boys. What was the relationship of the real world to the world of my experience? To annual rites like the Carnival parties I attended as a little boy, dressed as Aladdin or Pinocchio, in the beautiful frescoed rooms of Palazzo Ziino (the Ziinos being great friends of my family), along with all the other little Aladdins and Pinocchios from "nice" families? Or the Christmas receptions in Palazzo San Vincenzo, whose magnificent rooms were filled with the cream of Palermo's aristocracy? No wonder others regarded me as a member of a strange species!

The perplexity these thoughts caused me was increased by another encounter I had that summer of 1965. One day a schoolmate and friend named Nanni came to pick me up to go with him to San Martino, a beautiful place in the hills above Palermo. He'd had an argument with another boy named Marco Lupo and wanted me to help him get even. By the time we got to San Martino, however, I knew that this minor argument was not the real reason for the trip. In fact, Nanni was interested in a girl named Valeria, who was staying with Marco Lupo's family. When we arrived, Valeria came out to talk to us. With her was her friend Milli, Marco Lupo's sister. Milli's dark hair was tied in two little pigtails, emphasizing a small, pretty face that reminded me of a frightened bunny. Because my score on the *Maturità* exam had made me locally famous, Milli immediately asked my opinion on Kant's *Critique of Pure Reason*. And I, to my shame, was all too willing to give it to her.

We walked under the pine trees of San Martino, drinking in the resin-perfumed air, talking philosophy until we were invited up to the villa for cake. The house actually didn't belong to the Lupos; they had rented it while they were building their own villa. But it struck me as being very different from the houses I had always known. It was a house filled not only with jokes and laughter, but with real joy. It made me realize the extent to which the homes I had lived in had been beautiful, serene, and happy, yet never joyous. In this exciting house, the conversation leaped from philosophy to cinema to history to music as we ate our cake.

Very soon after this I traveled to London to study English for a month. One day the phone rang. It was Milli, who was staying in London too and had gotten my number from Nanni. Over the next few weeks, we explored the Tate Gallery, the British Museum, the Tower of London, the Victoria and Albert Museum. We walked in the parks. We went to the theater. We saw *My Fair Lady* and came out humming the tunes together. Milli's chief appeal was her normality. I was in love with it and with her. I always saw Milli home on the tube train—she lived in Watford, the last station on the Bakerloo line—and then returned in a state of euphoria to Finchley Street, where I lived in a huge house converted into a student hostel.

Milli's stay in London was over before mine, and on the night of her departure, I took her to a roaring party the Young Conservatives were throwing at Heathrow Airport and then put her on the plane. As a parting gift she gave me *The Charterhouse of Parma*. The next day I started feeling bad—so bad, in fact, that a few days later I ended up in Paddington Hospital. I had pneumonia, for the second time in my life. I called my parents, knowing they would be worried if they didn't hear from me for a long time, and I told them I would be away on a brief trip.

Was it the quality of my voice? Had my tone been too breezily nonchalant? Or was it some kind of sixth sense? Whatever it was that gave me away, my father and mother arrived at Paddington Hospital that very evening and immediately moved me to a private clinic, the Italian Hospital in Queen's Square, where I battled my illness for the next three weeks with my parents at my bedside, as I feverishly followed the fortunes of Stendhal's Fabrizio.

| | |

It was autumn when I returned to Palermo, just in time to register for the university. Since I had no particular preference of field and a test I had taken indicated that I was "qualified for all faculties," I followed the Orlando family tradition and decided to study law.

I also picked up my relationship with Milli, who had taken it upon herself to "normalize" me. People in the aristocratic world where I had lived shed easy tears over the starving children in Biafra, but knew nothing—or chose to know nothing—of the everyday tragedies of life among the underclass of Palermo. Through Milli I discovered that there were poor people and social outcasts in my own city. My first impulse, given my upbringing, was to pay someone to help them. Milli did the helping herself, and made nothing of her charitable acts. She was the sort of person who wrote to the

Pope telling him that the Church should do more for the poor. Writing the Pope! Unthinkable! She also taught me to swim—I who had spent two months of every summer of my life in a magnificent villa at the seaside, and was afraid of the water.

In 1968, after the earthquake in Sicily's Belice Valley killed hundreds and left thousands homeless, I took a truckload of clothes and other necessities to the disaster area as part of an effort organized by an association of former Gonzaga students. I didn't get close to the victims, but like others of my class, I could congratulate myself for having done what in the United States would be called "feel-good" work. But Milli was actively involved. She took me to meet a family who had lost both their home and their small shop. They had five children but couldn't support them any longer. Out of desperation they had decided to go to Germany as "guest workers," taking their oldest son with them. The other four children, aged from one to eight, they gave to Milli and me to keep. For the next three years, after settling the children in various homes, we acted as parents, looking after their material and emotional needs. When their parents had finally saved enough money to return to Sicily, it was Milli and I who introduced them to their youngest child, who no longer remembered them.

I never would have undertaken the fight against the Mafia just for the sake of law and order. I fought because I knew how the tentacles of the Mafia strangled the lives of common people. And I learned to care about these people in the first place because Milli opened my eyes to them.

| | |

I was the fourth generation of Orlandos to study law, but the first Orlando to do so at a school where his father was not only a professor but also the dean. This led to an awkward situation. Like most other major Italian universities in 1968 and 1969, Palermo was occupied by student protestors, and I was involved in this movement, but was regarded with suspicion by my comrades. After all,

I *was* the son of the dean. What my companions could in no way even vaguely imagine was the uncomfortable, almost surreal atmosphere at home when I sat down to our meals, perhaps coming there directly from a tumultuous demonstration. There I was, being served by Giuseppe in his white jacket and gloves, sitting beside my father whose building I had been occupying—and nothing was said. The subject hung heavily in the space between us, but was never put into words.

It was during this time that I also met a Jesuit priest, Father Ennio Pintacuda, brother of my professor of history and philosophy at Gonzaga and a man who would have a profound effect on my life. The Pintacuda family were country folk who came from Prizzi, the town where my grandfather was born, and all three of their sons became Jesuit priests. Because Sicily is in effect one big small town, the Pintacudas were people I had always known without knowing them well.

Father Pintacuda was a small man with a beak of a nose and a balding head that seemed to rest directly on his slightly hunched shoulders. Soft-spoken, with penetrating eyes staring out from behind large glasses, the priest conveyed shrewd intelligence and calculation. His attraction for me lay in his combination of moral imperatives and political pragmatism. For him social change was the art of the possible, a process of getting from one place to another.

In later years, his room at the Center for Social Studies, which he founded together with another Jesuit, was crammed with books, publications, magazines, clippings and newspapers, deposited in Leaning-Tower-of-Pisa-like piles on the shelves, on the floor, on the chairs. It was mesmerizing to watch him navigate through this benign chaos, his slender body dwarfed by his desk, small parts of which were periodically cleared to allow for writing. Father Pintacuda had, as I would discover, an obsession for documentation, for press clippings on a variety of subjects, which he would jealously preserve long after anybody else would have cleared them out.

He put this material to good use. In the years ahead, he would become a central figure in the fight against Cosa Nostra and corrupt politics, which for him were two sides of the same coin. A Christian Democrat by background, he was disgusted by the growing evidence of corruption in the party. Yet for obvious reasons he could not align himself with the Communists either, despite their courageous stand against the Mafia. So he steered his own course, forming a succession of organizations to build a cadre of energetic, educated individuals who with him would live their Christian convictions in their political actions.

I saw Father Pintacuda as someone with a compelling vision for the social world I was just then beginning to discover. He saw in me a potential disciple who could help him "remoralize" Sicilian society. In picking me for such a role, he was acting according to the old way of the Jesuits, who believe that if they can cultivate one "leader," they ultimately have the potential for influencing thousands of people. Pintacuda soon became a father figure for me in an area, politics, which had always been anathema to my real father. In time he would become my spiritual as well as my political advisor.

Influenced by Father Pintacuda, I worked with other students to found the Gonzaga Cultural-Artistic Association, whose aim was to open windows in our minds and force us to study issues outside our small, protected little slice of the world. This association would meet once a week at Father Pintacuda's room at Casa Professa, the Jesuit headquarters for Palermo and the whole of Sicily. Casa Professa is attached to one of the most extraordinary churches of Palermo, the Chiesa del Gesù (Church of Jesus), and a visitor entering it is bowled over by the overwhelming richness of the pink, white, black and ochre baroque marbles and stucco work.

Each member of the Gonzaga Cultural-Artistic Association was assigned a specific newspaper or magazine to read carefully, and every Monday we would meet in Father Pintacuda's room to discuss what we had learned. I was assigned *Rinascita*, the Communist Party weekly magazine, to study and report on, which I did faithfully during the next two years, always with a sense of unease. The magazine encouraged one to criticize all dominant concepts, except for those it rested upon. It struck me as being negative and destructive. Yet I understood that the task at hand was not just acquiring information, but probing political meanings and viewpoints. How did the Communists think about politics? Why had they fought against the Mafia? How did they try to embody their precepts in specific political positions?

My parents approved of my relationship with Father Pintacuda, regarding him as one of those *maîtres à penser* who would mold my mind in such a way as to make me useful and—if the truth were known—powerful. The only one who expressed any doubts was Milli, who saw in Father Pintacuda a certain Machiavellian quality. At a time when my relationship with Milli was troubled by wavering commitment on my part, the influence I allowed Father Pintacuda to exercise over me became another disquieting development for her. In 1967, after our umpteenth breakup, Milli decided to move to Catania, the other major Sicilian city, and go to school there. She visited Palermo off and on over the next two years, and we maintained our off-and-on relationship.

That same year, in the summer of 1967, I went to the University of Heidelberg to study German for a month on a *Ferienkurs*, a "holiday course." Why Heidelberg? Because it was the city where my father had studied in the early 1930s, and I remembered his after-dinner tales of the beerhouse Zum Zepp'l, where the young German students would challenge each other to duels aimed at slashing the opponent's cheek—the more slashes, the greater dexterity; the more scars, the greater proof of bravery. One of the first things I did upon arriving in Heidelberg, in fact, was to find Zum Zepp'l, which amazingly enough was still exactly as he had described it. In fact, my month in Germany was a sort of Proustian recovery of lost time—my father's time. I went to Unter Schloss Weg, a narrow street under the castle, where he had lived during his stay. I got at least a glimpse of that other self he had inhabited before he was my mother's husband and my father.

Upon returning to Palermo I still had Heidelberg on my mind, and I applied to the Ministry of Foreign Affairs for a scholarship to the Max Planck Institute. I was accepted and offered 800 deutsche marks a month (about 100 dollars at that time). It was a fraction of what I had lived on before, but I was enthusiastic not only about attending Heidelberg University full time, but about not being "the son of" for the first time in my life.

At first I stayed in the Students' Hostel, but soon decided that if I didn't go out to eat in restaurants and always ate—for the sum of one mark per meal—both lunch and dinner at the canteen, and if I did my own washing and ironing, I could afford a room at Palmbräuhaus, a sort of boarding house right in the old center of the city owned by an Italian who also ran a small trattoria called Sole d'Oro (The Golden Sun). Apart from the name of this restaurant, Heidelberg was cold and grey, and to guard against the dangers of a northern winter, my parents, still worried that I might die, had provided me with heavy coats, long underwear, a variety of jackets, lined gloves and even a fur hat. It was indeed very un-Mediterranean, but I loved Heidelberg for the freedom it offered—most of all, freedom from my own family and upbringing.

The revolutionary winds of 1968 were still blowing strongly in Germany, and the old wooden-beamed halls of the medieval university rang with the voices of some of Europe's most celebrated student leftists. One was Rudi Dutschke, who came up with the idea that radicals should stop toying with revolution and begin "the long march through the institutions." Another was Ulrike Meinhof, who believed the opposite and took revolution the next step into terrorism when she formed the Bader-Meinhof Gang. Yet I was more fascinated by two of our professors, whose lessons I never missed: Martin Heidegger and Hans Georg Gadamer, world-famous philosophers who were regarded as rather conservative.

I made friends with students of various nationalities and backgrounds. John, from California, had a Peugeot that was the envy of all the students, and we toured the German countryside in it every weekend. I became close friends with a Greek student who had fled from his country, then in the hands of the Colonels, and of course I made many German friends. One of them was one of my professors, Christian Tomuschat, responsible for the Italian section of Max Planck, with whom I played soccer every Thursday afternoon.

To me, these friends represented the wider world. To them, I represented Sicily. "Ah! Here comes the Mafioso!" they would joke. This was before the rise of the Corleonesi, the Mafia clan which a few years later would associate death and Palermo on front pages around the world. Yet even at this time, the Mafia was inching its way into the news, largely as a result of what came to be called the First Mafia War of the early 1960s (a name applied when we were in the middle of the second, far more apocalyptic conflict). Competition over the spoils of the Sack of Palermo led to a clash between various Mafia factions, culminating in a car bomb that killed seven police and bomb disposal experts in 1963.

I could have taken umbrage when my German friends called me "Mafioso," but I shrugged it off with a laugh. I was secure in the thought that the Mafia had nothing to do with me and, more importantly, I had nothing to do with it.

| | |

After two years at Heidelberg I returned to Palermo to take a position in the law school, feeling that I had finally thrown off most of my emotional shackles. My relationship with Father Pintacuda intensified, and under his influence I did a study called "Underdevelopment, Cultural Power and Mafia" for a 1970 conference organized by our Cultural-Artistic Association. It caused a scandal. This was not because I named names or made bold charges about who in Sicily's political world was complicit; nor did I discuss the Sack of Palermo or describe the Mafia's contamination of our culture. In fact, the paper was rather obtuse, dealing with the Mafia as if it were a tribe tucked away in some valley, which none of us had ever met. The study created a scandal simply because it was the first time ever that a non-Communist, a Catholic of the Gonzaga-Jesuit species, had written about this subject.

There was no road-to-Damascus epiphany. Like practically everyone else in Sicily, I had my insights by fits and starts. If I was a few steps ahead of most of my fellow citizens, it was only because of the moral prodding of a few people like Father Pintacuda and my own father. There was ample evidence of how dangerous it was to become too identified with this subject. There had been several Cassandras in our recent past: a handful of trade unionists, a brave Protestant pastor, a few Communists. Most of them were not merely ignored, but killed—not the highly public murders that lay a few years in the future, but almost inaudible thumps in the Sicilian night.

Still, I knew I was embarked on a path from which there would be no turning away. As a lawyer, I saw that the law was one place to wage the struggle. In the aftermath of the First Mafia War, a national Antimafia Commission had been established, and its findings encouraged a legal response by authorities. But while an individual Mafioso was brought to trial now and then, perhaps even jailed, there was no action directed at the Mafia per se. Father Pintacuda's view became mine as well: law enforcement was only part of the task ahead. In addition to trials and imprisonment, we somehow had to inject immunizing antibodies into Sicilian culture.

| | |

My intuition that the problem of the Mafia would be my life's work is probably what gave me confidence finally to propose to Milli, with whom I had maintained a fitful courtship while abroad. There were still tensions between us, but they seemed only to have strengthened our bond. Now that I had a job at the University of Palermo and would also be working in my father's law firm, it was time to get serious about our relationship.

Although she didn't belong to "our world," my parents had embraced Milli because of her loyalty and love for me. In choosing her I had gone against unwritten class laws, but so what? My mother too had "married beneath herself."

Our engagement was to be celebrated with a traditional *acchianata*, an old Sicilian term deriving from the verb *acchianare*, "to climb up." In the past, when two young people wished to be betrothed, custom dictated that the prospective groom's parents make a formal visit to the chosen bride's parents, going "up the stairs" to their living area. There would be cakes and a little Rosolio wine, and the parents of the young man would praise his morality, his capacity for hard work and his future financial prospects. The bride's parents, in turn, would praise her piety, her excellent housekeeping abilities and—often more important—what she would bring as dowry to her husband. In fact, the terms of the match had already been negotiated by a go-between before this meeting took place, but the ritual had to be respected in full. After a couple of hours, the bride and groom would be called in and formally "introduced" to each other, and then the engagement declared official.

My parents and I were to go to the Lupos' house, not for cakes and Rosolio wine but for dinner. My mother had given her own engagement ring, a superb diamond, to my brother Antonio's bride when he had become engaged. (The most rebellious and independent of the seven of us children, Antonio had married at the age of eighteen and was already a happy father.) For Milli, my mother went to Bulgari, the most prestigious Italian jeweler in Rome, and bought a ring that equaled in value and appearance the one she had already given away. Everything was fixed and confirmed. We were expected for dinner at the Lupos' home at nine.

At four o'clock in the afternoon of that memorable day, I picked up the phone in a panic and called Milli. "I don't want to become engaged," I blurted out. "I'm sorry but I can't do it…. I can't do it!"

She neither cried nor became upset. She didn't yell "You're crazy!" as she probably should have. She accepted it and immediately began thinking of what to do about the visit that had been so meticulously prepared. We agreed that I would tell my parents and she would tell hers that the engagement was off.

When I explained to my mother that I had changed my mind,

her reaction was mixed. "Marriage and an engagement are something very important, not to be entered into lightly," she said, "so if you're not sure, you shouldn't force it." But then, after a short pause, the *bon ton* of generations of Cammaratas came into play: "But there's a matter of the proprieties, of good manners. We've been invited to dinner by these people and we can't not go. The engagement is over, but we can't not go to dinner. We'll put the ring into the strongbox and bring Milli something else."

My mother had a rather lovely gold bracelet my father had given to her when I was born, to which she was very attached. Nonetheless, she carefully wrapped it in tissue paper and then the three of us went to dine with the Lupos.

Milli lived with her family in a beautiful, huge attic apartment with breathtaking views of the whole city. When we arrived, the house and the terrace were all lit up, and there were vases of flowers artistically placed in all the rooms and an elegantly laid table with an embroidered tablecloth. As we sat down to dinner, I felt we were in a situation that was almost comic. Six people eating excellent food (Milli's mother was a superb cook), drinking excellent wine and making charming conversation, although they no longer had any reason whatsoever to be having a formal dinner together.

That we shared the meal that evening and had fun doing so was probably responsible for the fact that a year later, in 1971, Milli and I finally *did* become engaged. This time the Bulgari diamond ring was rejected as unlucky and another was bought in its place. And having put aside all fears and uncertainties, we were married in the historic Church of the Magione, a wonderful Arab-Norman church situated in one of Palermo's ancient Arab quarters.

Milli wore a white dress with a white sable-trimmed hood, a delicate spray of white flowers in her hair framing her lovely face. Ours was *the* marriage of that season, attracting aristocrats, my Gonzaga friends, the important lawyers and professional bourgeoisie—all the men attired in swallowtails and top hats and the women all nearly as magnificent as Milli herself. The gossip columnists were kept busy for days describing the reception for hundreds of guests which was held at the Savoia Club, the most exclusive club of Palermo's nobility and still bearing the name of the exiled Italian royal family.

We honeymooned in Mexico for a month, then went to New York and Canada before returning home to settle in a small house where we would live for the next twenty-five years. We had two beautiful daughters whose pictures, like Milli's own, never appeared in the newspapers because of my fear that they would possibly be killed by the Mafia, which made no secret of the fact that it intended to kill me.

3

W hy did I become involved in the fight against the Mafia? Why did I start saying the word and repeating it until it became something like an obsession? There were small things: the murder of our doctor; my father saying he could not run for office because the Mafia had corrupted our politics. But the primary reason, as I later understood, was the awareness of my Sicilian identity. My family and Father Pintacuda set the process of such an awareness in motion. It was Father Pintacuda in particular who not only said the word "Mafia" but began to apply a definition. It was he who led me to realize that the Mafia was not just a dark fantasy, but a real sociological phenomenon. He did not do this because of some abstract or perverse interest in the subject (which for some Sicilians is akin to an interest in pornography), but because he was interested in the growth of community and the development of democracy, and he knew that the Mafia stood in the way of both.

Father Pintacuda's interest in Cosa Nostra intensified at the very time that the organization was becoming virtually invisible. The combination of the First Mafia War and the national Antimafia Commission that followed had forced the Mafia to lie low and regroup during the early 1970s. This was also the time of terrorism in Italy, and dealing with the Red Brigades monopolized the attention of the authorities. (Indeed, the situation became so desperate that civil servants allegedly contacted imprisoned Mafiosi such as Tommaso Buscetta, who later became the first Mafia informant, in an attempt to convince them to infiltrate and give information on the terrorists who were also jailed.) But while Italy's attention was directed elsewhere, the Mafia was not asleep; it was morphing into a different organization with different objectives. After the heroin link between Marseilles and the United States— the so-called French Connection—was broken in 1974, the Sicilian Mafia moved silently into the vacuum. Before, it had smuggled cigarettes and other contraband. Now it was setting up heroin refineries and using these networks, along with its genetic connection to the American Cosa Nostra, to begin a traffic that would make Sicily the narcotics capital of the world.

The capital of that capital was Palermo. Becoming involved in the politics of the city was a natural consequence of the social action Father Pintacuda advocated. And in Sicily, becoming involved in politics meant becoming involved in the Christian Democratic Party.

I was, to say the least, ambivalent about it. The Christian Democrats had become established in the postwar era as a bulwark against communism, including the Eurocommunism that the West regarded as the first step down a slippery slope. Leaders and governments came and went, but the Christian Democrats were eternal. Yet during the time of its hegemony, the party had become smug, oppressive, inefficient, cliental, morally compromised— everything that made me, a committed Christian who should have been a natural constituent, reject them. This was before the web connecting the CDs to the Mafia had been diagrammed; though even without such revelations, it was clear that the party limited the range of opinion and narrowed the spectrum of the permissible so that it was impossible to incorporate any sort of idealism into the political process it controlled.

But then, because of terrorism and economic concerns, Italians (but not Sicilians) rebuffed the Christian Democrats in the national elections of 1975. The party plummeted to its historical low point since the end of the Second World War. Father Pintacuda and I saw this as a sign of hope. Perhaps the party could be reborn into a politics that was both truly Christian and truly democratic. This hope was strengthened by the presence on the Sicilian political scene of a man named Piersanti Mattarella.

Although twelve years older than I, Mattarella too was a professor at the university and therefore my colleague. He had done an apprenticeship in my father's law firm, and the first time I had met him was when my family was invited to his wedding. But apart from that occasion and good wishes at Christmas and Easter, we had never socialized.

Piersanti was the son of Bernardo Mattarella, one of the most powerful Christian Democrats in Sicily during the postwar era. Bernardo's star had fallen rapidly, however, after his name had appeared in a report by the Communist minority of the Parliamentary Antimafia Commission as the man "who had striven to absorb Mafia forces into the Christian Democrats so as to use them as an instrument of power." Piersanti *never* spoke of his father. It was clearly an extremely painful subject for him, and indeed, the pain became almost tangible on occasions when somebody, with words or looks, would insinuate: "*You* are different...." Still, his father's and his party's experiences were probably responsible for Piersanti's uncompromising desire to cleanse the Christian Democrats of any such connections.

When I got to know Piersanti Mattarella, he was commissioner for budget in the Sicilian regional government and author of a proposal for a thoroughgoing reform of the outdated regional bureaucracy. Here was a man proposing the laws that desperately needed to be passed if Sicily was to enter the modern age. I felt that we spoke the same language, the language of a new administrative culture—functional, modern, European.

One morning in early 1976, I visited Mattarella in his office. He was a tall, blue-eyed, elegant man with a profound dignity. As I stuttered out my desire to become involved in his political work, he looked at me and said, "You mustn't worry." He might have been referring to the party's past and present situation, as well as to my obvious unease, but in fact I stopped worrying on the spot. Piersanti was gentle and soft-spoken, inspiring one with a sense of confidence. Even though the Sicilian political scene was degraded, he considered politics itself a noble art. He was so sure of himself that he never acted as if he needed to have your consent, yet he always deeply respected your dissent. He was a true and truly devout Catholic, and instinctively a shy man with a gift of quiet courage.

At the end of our first conversation, I felt it was a *duty* to do what I could to support his effort to cleanse the Sicilian political system, so I finally took out a party card. In my mind, however, it was very clear that I had not become a member of the Christian Democratic Party so much as the Piersanti Mattarella party.

| | |

Piersanti had formed a group called *Politica*, composed of young professionals like myself who met once a week under his guidance to discuss current problems and their possible solutions. It was a group obsessed with politics, but our discussions were really about ethics, as was indicated by the titles of the conferences and debates we organized: "Faith and Politics," "A Christian's Commitment in Politics," "Ethics and Politics."

Father Ennio Pintacuda was close to our movement and was frequently invited to speak at our conferences or debates. This in spite of the fact that Piersanti was suspicious of the Jesuits and what he regarded as their hidden agendas; he was much closer to the Franciscans and the Salesians, seeing their humility as a truer reflection of Christ's message of love.

Mattarella's first big move came at the Christian Democrats' 1976 regional congress, held at the Hotel Zagarella, a modern, multistoried building owned by Ignazio and Nino Salvo, cousins connected to Salvo Lima and Vito Ciancimino and the Sack of Palermo. The Salvos were a metaphor for what was wrong with our society. They had acquired incredible wealth after getting themselves named tax collectors for Sicily, a post which entitled them to keep 10 percent of all taxes they brought in! They had invested in real estate, vineyards, hotels—all of it networked in a complex way with Mafia holdings. The Salvos were known as "grand electors" of the Christian Democratic Party and famed for saying of certain political figures, "That lemon has been fully squeezed," after which the lemon would not be reelected.

At the 1976 congress, Piersanti caused a furor by refusing to include his name in the *listone*, the "big slate" of candidates for Christian Democratic Party delegates headed by Vito Ciancimino, who, since presiding over the Sack of Palermo, had alternately dominated the city's politics and disappeared into the background. Defying Ciancimino, Piersanti insisted on running a minority slate of his own candidates, my own name among them. (The rule was that any list must get at least 10 percent of the vote to have representation.) Despite the fact that Ciancimino bought off one of Piersanti's delegates at the last minute, he was unable to keep us from getting the necessary votes, and so we became a presence in the party.

We worked hard over the next year to expand our influence, telling voters that we would clean up the party and make it accountable. And in 1978, Mattarella was chosen president of the Sicilian Region by a vote of our parliament, and I became his legal advisor. He took office at the same time that one of the most terrible events in recent Italian history was beginning to unfold. On the morning of March 16, the Red Brigades kidnapped President Aldo Moro, leaving behind the bullet-riddled bodies of his five bodyguards. The news immediately interrupted all radio and television programs and swept through the entire country within minutes. As soon as I heard it, I rushed to Piersanti's office.

"This is the end for President Moro," I said.

"This is the end for me as well," Piersanti answered grimly.

I wasn't sure what he meant. It was true that he looked to Moro as his point of reference within the national Christian Democratic Party. But what was the relationship between Moro's kidnapping and Piersanti? He didn't tell me that on the same morning he had received his first death threats—not from the Red Brigades, but from the Mafia.

The fifty-five days that followed were filled with anguish for the fate of Aldo Moro and discussions at the highest level on whether to negotiate with the terrorists. Then on May 9, Moro's body was found in a red Renault, deliberately parked equidistant between the Christian Democrat and Communist headquarters in Rome. The country reeled under the shock.

All this was a godsend to the Mafia. Italy was preoccupied with rising Cold War tensions and especially with terrorism. During the 1970s there were some three thousand acts of violence, less than 10 percent of them in Sicily. As the Red Brigades soaked up police attention, other issues receded in importance. It was no accident that the Antimafia Commission, which had been keeping tabs on Cosa Nostra since the First Mafia War of the early 1960s, was now disbanded. This left the false impression that it had taken care of business—despite the chilling conclusion of its final report: "There exists a criminal structure which, in putting up an impenetrable wall to noncompromised authorities, operates for the support and protection of Mafia criminal activities."

What the commission didn't say—and didn't know—was that the Mafia was now supplying close to half of the heroin smuggled into the United States. It had opened a number of refineries in Sicily by the end of the 1970s. Between 1976 and 1980, when the first of these refineries were discovered, several metric tons of pure heroin were exported, worth an estimated $600 million in profits.

| | |

My office as legal advisor to the president was on the first floor of Palazzo d'Orleans, once owned by the Duke of Paris, a beautiful building on the square behind the Norman Palace. Mattarella's rooms were on the second floor, and I spent as much time there as in my own office.

In the two years that I worked as Piersanti's legal advisor, we designed several laws, the most important of which was a law that transferred the responsibility for a large part of the regional budget from the regional commissioners to the cities of Sicily. It was a revolutionary law in its way. Over the years, the position of regional commissioner had become too powerful, able to move millions of dollars in one direction rather than another on the strength of a single signature. Without checks and balances, the position had become vulnerable to Mafia penetration. The aim of our law was to put this money directly into the hands of the various municipalities that were supposed to be the beneficiaries of the spending, thus making the sum spent with a single stroke of the pen less appetizing. I worked hard on the details of each article of the law, which was finally approved by the regional parliament.

Piersanti was also responsible for passing a law forcing Sicily to comply with building standards that had been in effect in the rest of Italy for over a decade. Such a measure seemed innocuous enough, but it was a step onto dangerous ground. No past president of the Region had dared become involved with building rules and regulations of Sicily, and especially of Palermo, where they were exclusively controlled by the Mafia and its front men in the political world.

Without any oversight, the city of Palermo, for instance, had let six contracts for the construction of six schools in six different districts of the city. For each contract only one construction company submitted a bid. This would be unusual in any city, but it was astounding in a city where there was such a hunger for work and where the construction business—however hideous its product—was flourishing. Piersanti commissioned an investigation into the circumstances of such deals and discovered, without much effort, that the six construction companies that submitted winning bids were connected to the *capimafia* of the six districts where the schools were to be built. When Piersanti's advisors discussed this discovery with him, I had to keep myself from smiling. How could those bosses be so stupid as not to permit another company to submit a bid, if for no other reason than to create the appearance of open competition? My amusement showed how ignorant I still was of the Mafia mentality.

Slowly I began to understand the principle of territorial control. Engaging in a charade of fairness was not the Mafia's way. Egregiousness was exactly the point. When its own company was the only one submitting a bid, the Mafia provided an object lesson about sovereignty. Everybody could see that the dominion of these six bosses was absolute and not subject to any bourgeois niceties.

One morning Mattarella and I were on our way to a meeting when we ran into a man named Mignosi who was investigating the school contracts. He looked haggard and his voice was tense.

"Mr. President, I need to speak to you."

Maria Trizzino, Mattarella's chief of staff, broke in: "Mr. Mignosi is extremely worried, Mr. President."

"Why?" Piersanti asked.

"Well," Mrs. Trizzino continued hesitantly, "he has discovered some very peculiar things. He's afraid that somebody is going to make him pay for it."

"Make *him* pay?" Piersanti asked. "Why him? Everyone knows that *I* am the one who wants this investigation. They should make *me* pay." With gestures such as this he was protecting the rest of us, although this made him the target of the Mafia.

| | |

One afternoon, Piersanti and I were driving to Cefalù, the famous coastal town east of Palermo. We were whizzing along a straight stretch of road with the sea on our left, when I opened my briefcase and took out some documents I had written for Piersanti to sign. They concerned a law we were drafting to increase the number of inspectors of public works in Sicily and force them to rotate regularly from one city to another. This would prevent these extremely powerful figures who decided how public construction monies were spent from being corrupted by Mafia-owned companies. This new measure did not receive much publicity, but like the investigation of the six schools, it was a dagger aimed at the heart of the status quo.

"Piersanti, you *do* know what you are signing, don't you?" I asked.

"Yes, of course."

"Don't you think it can be dangerous?"

"We're only doing our duty," he shrugged. "No more and no less."

His answer was casual, meant to reassure me. But it didn't have that effect. Before, perhaps, one might have assumed that a high-ranking public official like Piersanti would be safe. Traditionally, the Mafia's credo had been: Always within the state; never openly against the state. But Cosa Nostra was changing. It would take time to understand how profoundly, but it was already clear that things were different.

In years to come there would be an outbreak of nostalgia for the "old" Mafia—the Mafia of rules and honor among thieves; the romanticized Mafia that never harmed women or children. Such a Mafia never existed, of course. The leaders of what would be seen as the "old" Mafia were ruthless men. One was Stefano Bontate, a boss of Palermo, who became notorious for arriving an hour late for a meeting and flippantly telling those waiting, "Sorry to be late. I had to change a tire and strangle Stefano Giacona." Another was Gaetano Badalamenti, a boss of Cinisi, a locale near the airport which had become increasingly important with the growing traffic in narcotics. Badalamenti had famously slapped a member of Parliament in the 1960s when the man failed to produce results. And when Giuseppe Impastato, the son of a "man of honor," rebelled against his family's ties with the Mafia and, as an anchorman for a local radio station, began calling the old boss mocking names, Badalamenti had him murdered despite the pleas of the young man's father.

Yet notwithstanding their viciousness, bosses such as Bontate and Badalamenti had maintained the obsession with invisibility that had always guided the Mafia. For them, no news was good news; Cosa Nostra must work from within and not upset the social equilibrium of which it was such a crucial part. Most of all, it must coexist with authority rather than challenge it directly.

But the drug trade had tested this worldview. The profits were huge, creating an arrogant grandiosity and opening a window onto a world without limits. Moreover, a new and particularly homicidal faction, amoral even by Mafia standards, was rising inside Cosa Nostra. These were the Corleonesi, named after the town of Corleone where they arose. The godfather of this faction was Luciano Leggio, the man who had taken control of the Corleonesi after murdering my family doctor. A psychopath who carried a bayonet-like knife with him to settle quarrels, Leggio had finally been sent to prison in 1974, but had continued to wield power through two even more ferocious henchmen. One was Bernardo Provenzano, known as *u tratturi*, "the Tractor," because of his machine-like capacity for slaughter. The other, shrewder and more dangerous, was a short, beady-eyed man name Salvatore ("Totò") Riina, *la belva*, "the Beast."

The Corleonesi were derided as *viddani*, "peasants," by Bontate, Badalamenti and the other more sophisticated Mafiosi of the cities. These big-city bosses felt more vulnerable to law enforcement and wanted to draw as little notice to themselves as possible. Since the First Mafia War they had dominated the *cupola*, or Commission, the ruling body composed of the most powerful and authoritative *capifamiglia* ("family bosses"), through which the entire Sicilian Mafia set policy and kept the peace in Sicily's western provinces. But the Corleonesi were not interested in accommodation or Cosa Nostra's perverse version of constitutionality. They made no nice distinctions between symbols of authority and enemies inside the Mafia itself when choosing their targets. Slowly they began to alter our reality.

There was a hierarchy of homicide for Cosa Nostra. A "normal" killing—of a *picciotto* who had misbehaved, for instance—lay within the authority of the *capofamiglia*. An "excellent" killing—of some local politician or law enforcement official, say—required permission from the Commission. A "most excellent" killing, of a major personality, was at times decided upon by a Commission enlarged to include bosses representing the other Sicilian provinces.

In 1977, according to this protocol, the Corleonesi had asked the Commission for permission to kill Giuseppe Russo, a colonel in the *carabinieri* who had been investigating contracts issued for waterworks outside of Corleone. Permission had been denied: the last thing the Mafia wanted was to begin killing policemen. The Corleonesi had killed Russo anyway, shooting him while he was on vacation and then trying to kill his reputation too by circulating innuendoes that he had been done in by the jealous husband of a woman he was sleeping with. But, at least on this, they failed—a few years later a gold medal was awarded to Colonel Russo's memory in recognition of his bravery.

The next "excellent cadaver" (the phrase came from the title of a film by the Italian director Francesco Rosi) was Boris Giuliano, deputy police chief of Palermo, who was shot on July 21, 1979. I had met him a few years earlier when I was working in my father's law firm. At that time, the papers had printed a false rumor that my father intended to run for mayor, which led to crank phone calls and some explicit death threats. I called Giuliano, who came to see me and suggested some security precautions. Then he was astute and confident; now he was dead, shot as he began sipping his morning coffee at an espresso bar. He was the first person I had ever known, however casually, to meet with a violent and brutal death. From newspaper reports, I learned that at the time of his murder, Giuliano was following the trail of a suitcase full of money that had been found at Palermo's Punta Raisi Airport—narcodollars not just from drug trafficking, but from refineries which he was apparently the first to have discovered on Sicilian soil.

Next it was Judge Cesare Terranova, who had just returned to Palermo as a prosecutor after some years in Rome as member of Parliament for the Communist Party. Terranova was fearless, having drawn up indictments of the most important Mafiosi, including Luciano Leggio, who had been apprehended after the First Mafia War. He had been a member of the Antimafia Commission, thundering at the "halo of untouchability" that the bosses' political connections gave them, and he was one of the first nemeses of Cosa Nostra to "follow the money" by investigating banking and financial records.

On September 25, a few weeks after Giuliano's murder, Terranova got into his car with an aide. Three killers came alongside and riddled the car with shot, and then to ensure that Terranova was indeed dead, gave him a coup de grâce in his neck.

Terranova's death required a more complex reading than Giuliano's, which could be seen as a deadly moment in the eternal game of cops and robbers. Terranova had played a political role for many years, and had also been a judge; now he was returning to his robe. His killing was a confirmation that the Mafia was no longer willing to live within limits.

| | |

A couple of months before Boris Giuliano's death, Piersanti decided that it was time to try to "open" Sicily—for so many years closed in upon itself—to investments by the wealthy northern Europeans. Such a strategy made good economic sense. Development would create wealth, with all its expectations for an orderly life. It would also begin to break power away from the Mafia. He envisioned Sicilian development, not as a few large industrial installations—often cause of pollution and environmental damage—but as many small and medium-sized industries such as those which had helped the north of Italy to flourish.

For the first time, a president of the Sicilian Region met with the heads of the Lombardian Industrialists' Association. (Lombardy is the region in northern Italy of which Milan is the capital.) Next we found another area that closely corresponded to Piersanti's idea of development, and was rich and successful: Baden-Württemberg in Germany. Because I had studied there and spoke German, Piersanti decided to send me for a first meeting with entrepreneurs there.

I made the case for Sicily well enough that a few weeks later Piersanti and I both went to Stuttgart, Germany. This visit was enormously successful. Piersanti met with Lothar Späth in the office of the president of Baden-Württemberg and agreed that some time after the New Year, agreements would be finalized for major German investments. We left for home on a contrail of euphoria. What possibilities! What promising future prospects of investment and work—buildings that would be habitable and roads that would go somewhere—for the Sicilian people!

In 1980, the Feast of the Epiphany fell on a Sunday. For Italians, the Epiphany signals the end of the Christmas–New Year festive season. (*Epifania tutte le feste si porta via*, goes the popular saying: "Epiphany takes all the holidays away with it.") It was around one in the afternoon, and I was wandering around the house in my robe, sipping with pleasure my third cup of coffee, when I happened to glance at the television. The program was one of those inane shows broadcast on Sunday mornings in Italy, but just as I was turning away, my eye was caught by words scrolling across the bottom of the screen: "The ex-president of the Sicilian Region, Piersanti Mattarella has been seriously wounded!" I was frozen to the spot. Then the message scrolled again, subtly changed: "The ex-president of the Sicilian Region, Piersanti Mattarella, has been mortally wounded!"

My brain seemed to be incapable of reaction. It balked at the prefix "ex." It was a mistake, a typo. Piersanti wasn't an "ex"; he *was* the president of the Sicilian Region. But the words kept coming: "Piersanti Mattarella shot in his car in Via Libertà."

I threw on some clothes and hurried to Villa Sofia, the hospital where they had taken him. There I discovered that he was not "mortally wounded" but dead. He had been killed as he was about to go to Sunday Mass in his car—without his driver, whom he had given the day off to spend with his wife and children. Piersanti had been killed in front of his wife; she had even begged the killer not to shoot him.

I didn't know what to do; I didn't know where to go; I didn't know whom to trust, whom to fear. Instinctively, along with Piersanti's other colleagues, I straggled into the office. We all hoped that tidying some papers or doing some other routine work would wake us from this nightmare. But Piersanti had always been a detail man. Not a single document or paper was out of place. There was nothing to do.

Piersanti's body lay in state in his rooms on the second floor of Palazzo d'Orleans. On the wall above his coffin, there was a beautiful picture depicting the clash between two cavaliers, a traditional Sicilian scene rendered by a Sicilian painter from a traditional Sicilian town—Corleone. For a while, Piersanti was surrounded only by those who had worked with him. But then something unusual happened. Hundreds of Sicilian families, with their children, filed in front of Piersanti's coffin to pay homage—mothers with strollers, fathers holding the hands of their sons and daughters.

The day of Piersanti's funeral was grey, wet and dreary. We friends shouldered his coffin, our faces washed by tears and rain at the same time. In the packed cathedral, the cardinal archbishop of Palermo, Salvatore Pappalardo, spoke of evil. None of us imagined that this was to be the first of many terrible funerals in that cathedral, or that the cardinal's words would grow in strength and become a torch to light our way through the darkness into which the Mafia had plunged us.

Piersanti was killed on January 6. The next day I received a phone call from Stuttgart: "We just heard the news. We are extremely sorry, but at this point all our agreements are annulled."

All relations with the Baden-Württemberg entrepreneurs were cut off. All relations between the Lombardian industrialists and Sicily died before they could be born.

4

The first phone call claiming responsibility for Piersanti's assassination came from a fascist terrorist group. We couldn't completely discount the possibility; Piersanti had made vague openings to the Left. But so had Aldo Moro, and he had been assassinated by the left-wing Red Brigades. The more likely possibility was the Mafia, which never claimed responsibility for any of its deaths. Piersanti's hostility to Ciancimino and all that Ciancimino stood for was well known. Piersanti's hostility to the Salvo cousins, who also came from Salemi, a small village in the same province of Trapani from which Piersanti's own family came, was also well known.

These were the men, together with their associates and supporters, that Piersanti had picked as his enemies. And now it was clear that this correlation of forces had killed him—not so much for what he had done, as for who he was and what he might do as he continued to probe the connection between finance, construction and politics. In this sense, Piersanti was and remains the most illustrious public figure to have been preemptively murdered.

Before I had seen a clear path: working to make the Christian Democratic Party habitable for people not willing to live in a state of collusion with Cosa Nostra. Now I felt as if I had lost my bearings. A close friend of mine, Baron Giancarlo Valenti, was one of the few who understood how the death of Piersanti affected me.

He tried to break through my depression, but couldn't make contact. One evening he came to visit, bringing with him a compass to which he had attached some twine.

"Maybe this will help you find your way," he said as he looped it around my neck.

Two months later, Giancarlo was returning from the country on a rainy night when his car skidded on the highway and fell into a ravine, killing him immediately. He left me his magnificent house, the Villa Virginia, where Milli and I and our daughters eventually moved.

|　|　|

In 1980, elections were scheduled for the Palermo Municipal Council. Piersanti's brother, Sergio, and other Mattarella friends and followers urged me to pick up the fallen standard.

"Luca, you have to stand as a candidate for the council," Sergio insisted. "These are the first elections after Piersanti's death. Piersanti's killers must be made to see that they may have killed him, but not his ideas."

I agreed to run and immediately paid a courtesy call on Salvatore Mantione, the outgoing mayor. He was a pharmacist by training and in fact was president of the Pharmacists' Association of Palermo, and he invited me to his home. Although it was early April, it was already very warm. I was ushered into the stuffy living room. Through chinks in the lowered wooden blinds and half-drawn linen curtains, the sun drew patterns on the floor. An old man, swathed in his dressing gown, appeared and courteously indicated an armchair. It was one of those ritualized Sicilian moments.

"May I offer you a cup of coffee?" he asked as we both sat at the same time.

"Please."

As he stirred his sugar in his cup, sitting in the half-shadow, he gave me a look of curiosity touched by compassion.

"Why on earth are you doing this?" he asked. "Entering politics in Palermo? Look what being the mayor of Palermo has done to me!"

I looked at his melancholy face and the message of pessimism engraved on it, and realized that this man who looked so drawn was actually in his middle years, prematurely aged by the job. I felt like changing my mind on the spot.

If I had been just another Christian Democratic candidate, I would have been deluged with offers of "help." But I was backed by Piersanti's friends and represented his philosophy, so no one offered any help and I requested none. In the early stages of my campaign, a wise old Palermitan, speaking in Sicilian dialect, warned me, "Professor, you are respected. Not many people know you, but those who know you will vote for you, and you'll be elected. But you'll go as far as the Baby Luna and no further."

The Baby Luna was a bar on a bridge that crosses the Oreto River—at the time a malodorous, polluted body of water separating the city from some of the highest-density Mafia suburbs such as Brancaccio, Ciaculli, and Croceverde Giardini. And indeed, when the returns of the election started coming in, it seemed as if I was going to be among the top vote getters; but when the votes from the districts beyond the Oreto began to arrive, I plummeted downward in the standings. The old man had seen right. I had gone as far as the Oreto River and no further. I was elected—but just barely.

Like most citizens, I had always avoided the Palazzo delle Aquile, our city hall and symbol of what was rotten in Palermo. Now I was taking my place in that magnificent council chamber. Going up its grand marble staircase, I looked out of the large, arched back windows onto one of Palermo's loveliest sights, the Arab-Norman Church of San Cataldo, with its characteristic three small brick-red domes and beside it the church known as La Martorana, with its twelfth-century bell tower.

It was comforting to look at the scenery, but when I went inside to try to carry out my duties as a councilor, I found myself in a surreal atmosphere. I remember one early meeting where a multi-million-dollar construction contract for public housing was to be discussed and voted on. I said what to me seemed obvious: that a contract should be put out for public bid. The head of the Christian Democrat group of councilors immediately quoted a respected jurist who had given an authoritative opinion that the contract could be awarded without such a bidding process. (I soon discovered that there was always an "authoritative" jurist prepared to "authoritatively" defend the positions of a Mafioso). I indicated that I wanted to make a short speech on why I planned to vote against such an approach. Just as I stood up, another councilor pulled my sleeve and hissed: "Watch it! They shoot!"

At first I thought he was joking, but then I realized that the words were a real warning. I was shaken. I did go ahead and speak, but I did not attack the process, as I had planned to do. I spoke and voted against it, but that was all. I kept hearing those words: they shoot! I knew they did, of course, having seen Piersanti's body. With time, I would learn that my timorousness might have been a natural response, but it was a tactical mistake. It is better to oppose the Mafia loudly rather than equivocally. The Mafia knows what your position is before you even announce it, but if you shout your opposition loudly, the non-Mafiosi will also know, and they may save your life.

| | |

The attack on representatives of the state, which had started with the assassinations of Colonel Russo, Boris Giuliano, Judge Terranova and then Piersanti, did not stop.

Emanuele Basile was a captain of the *carabinieri* who had picked up Giuliano's investigation of drugs shipped out of the Punta Raisi airport. He had traced the trafficking to the mainland town of Bologna (Italy was in the middle of an epidemic of heroin addiction) and to an uncle of Totò Riina's and a cousin of Luciano Leggio's. In May 1980, just as he had begun to turn his investigation from the narcotics themselves to the banking records of the men he was following, Basile, with his four-year-old daughter in his arms, watched a procession connected with the Feast of the Holy Crucifix in the hill town of Monreale. Three gunmen approached from behind and pumped a half-dozen shots into his back.

A few months later, when everyone who could had made up an excuse that would allow them to escape to the seashore, Gaetano Costa, Palermo's chief prosecutor, braved the suffocating heat to go out before dinner and buy some magazines and books to take with him on the holiday he was beginning with his family the following day. A solitary killer followed him from his home and, in one of the city's central streets, emptied his gun into Costa's face and head. Costa was so disfigured that an hour elapsed before the authorities realized that they were faced with yet another illustrious corpse—in this case, of a man who many years previously had began to warn members of the Antimafia Commission that local officials and the contracts they signed should be carefully scrutinized because they were "regular only in appearance."

So little had Gaetano Costa trusted the majority of his colleagues that he would frequently arrange to meet "by chance" with one of the few colleagues he *did* trust, Rocco Chinnici, head of the other prosecutorial presence in the city, the Investigating Magistrates' Office.* Costa and Chinnici would meet in an elevator and discuss the investigations they were each pursuing while going up to the top floor and back down again.

Hastily the Christian Democrat group of city councilors convened to draw up a statement on Costa's assassination to be presented to the council for approval. Some councilors whom I had already identified as puppets of Ciancimino strongly objected to

---

* Italian prosecutors and judges are all "magistrates," a profession for which they qualify through a national competition. In the course of their career they may easily pass from the role of prosecutor to that of judge or vice versa. The Investigating Magistrates' Office of Palermo (Chinnici) had the task of reviewing cases presented by the Office of the Prosecutor (Costa), conducting further investigations, and indicting or acquitting the defendant. Its investigating magistrates would be in the forefront of the antimafia struggle.

the use of the word "Mafia" in the document. They insisted that it be replaced by the word "criminality," as in "such criminality as there unfortunately is in any large city." The discussion became quite heated. The reaction that most struck me was that of a young, ambitious councilor named Giuseppe Insalaco, who throughout his political career had been close to the Mafia.

"How do these guys reason?" Insalaco suddenly exploded. "They don't want to use the word 'Mafia'? Why? Have they got some Don Peppino, *capomafia* of some minor district, who's worried about this word? Haven't they yet woken up to the fact that Don Peppinos and their bosses can't keep this word from being used any longer?"

Coming from Insalaco, this was a stark indication that the time for denying the Mafia's existence had ended. Before, using this word was tantamount to drawing a line in the sand. Now it could no longer be denied that there was a Mafia, although it was still impossible to find anyone who belonged to it.

| | |

For almost a year I struggled on as a member of the city council, feeling ever more useless and frustrated. Working with Father Pintacuda, I tried to figure a way to inch forward the issues of morality in our government and culture. We decided to organize a debate, together with Pio La Torre, head of the Sicilian Communist Party and member of Parliament, on the subject of "Politics and the Mafia." It took place in the municipal hall in Monreale, a small town in the hills above Palermo famed for its cathedral, an architectural jewel box containing some of Italy's most magnificent mosaics and a peerless cloister in pure Arab-Norman style. During the event, La Torre attacked my party and Vito Ciancimino, by name, as being the point at which the two terms in the debate converged. I was deeply anticommunist and knew that the Communist Party had its own nefarious reasons for attacking the Mafia— discrediting the party in power—but still it was on the right side of the issue.

Pio La Torre challenged me to sign the petition he was circulating against the Cruise missiles that were to be installed in Comiso, a small town in eastern Sicily. I agreed, mainly because I thought the presence of a military base would further diminish the poor economic prospects of that depressed area. Afterward, the reaction of the secretary of the Sicilian Christian Democratic Party was so violent that it left me speechless. I was attacked publicly and in the local press. Dissent, even on international issues not directly tied to the Mafia, disturbed the climate of acquiescence and stagnation that defined Sicily at this time. Any interruption of the status quo was forbidden.

I was returning to Palermo from Rome one afternoon and by chance found myself at the airport with Pio La Torre, who was making the same trip. La Torre was a man with extraordinary personal charisma, part of which came from his frankness and his ability to cut to the heart of an issue. He was on the right side not only of the Mafia issue, but many others as well, having fought for the enfranchisement of peasants and agricultural workers, many of whom were still living in almost feudal conditions into the 1960s and 1970s. La Torre was one of the first to understand the danger represented by the enormous illicit wealth accumulated by Mafiosi and he had introduced a bill in Parliament allowing the state to confiscate the assets, bank accounts and properties proved to be fruit of this criminal activity. This was the most audacious assault yet on Cosa Nostra. Even more radical was the bill's provision that merely being a member of the Mafia be treated as a criminal offense.

When I saw La Torre at the airport in Rome, I laughed and said, "Have you seen what happens when one sides with you?"

"No, what?"

"This very day, I've been violently attacked by the secretary of my party because I signed your petition on the missiles."

Torre smiled and said, "And they accuse *us* of being undemocratic!"

| | |

When the body count began to climb in 1981, we were all with the illustrious corpses of the men who had tried to bring the Mafia to justice. But most of the deaths involved Mafiosi themselves as what we now called the Second Mafia War broke out all around us.

The First Mafia War had involved pitched battles between the opposing factions. The second was a stealth war, whose commander in chief, Totò Riina, had been dismissed by the smoother big-city capos as an uncouth murderer. (Later on, when he was finally apprehended, Riina would plead that he was a simple man, an *analfabeto* or illiterate—proving his point by incorrectly using this noun, one of the few in Italian that always ends in a feminine "a.") But he was a man of ferocious ambition, thirsty for power and firmly determined to get absolute control over Cosa Nostra, including the avalanche of profits it had started making from drugs. Law enforcement authorities were not the only ones standing in his way. The overly cautious big-city bosses were also a problem with their credo of "Never against the state; always within the state." And so he moved against both.

The first sign of what the Corleonesi were up to had come in 1978 when Giuseppe Di Cristina, boss of the eastern Sicilian town of Riesi, went to police to tell them about this sect that had killed Colonel Russo and would kill others, and was beginning to eliminate its rivals in Cosa Nostra. He also predicted his own death, which came to pass not long after. Among other items authorities found in Di Cristina's pockets was a slip of paper with the telephone number of the fabulously wealthy Salvo cousins, pillars of the Christian Democratic world. But they did not follow up on this clue or on Di Cristina's warnings about the Corleonesi.

The deaths of Piersanti and the others had proved Di Cristina right in one of his warnings. And now the more invisible deaths of Mafiosi associated with Badalamenti, Bontate and the other "traditional" bosses proved the other part.

Most of Riina's intramural murders occurred outside Palermo's field of vision. The corpses were not illustrious in a social or moral sense, and most were never found, becoming *lupara bianca* disappearances (*lupara* for the sawed-off shotgun traditionally used to shoot the wolves that once roamed the Sicilian countryside, and *bianca* or "white" for the notion that there is no blood in a body that is never found). Rather than wage a street war like the previous Mafia conflict of the 1960s, Riina worked to peel away supporters from his rivals' forces, letting them see the inevitability of the Corleonesi.

Gaetano Badalamenti, who with Stefano Bontate and Totò Riina had controlled Cosa Nostra during the 1970s, left the country. A boss named Michele Greco, whose Mafia family had entered into an alliance with the Corleonesi, was co-opted into Badalamenti's place. Greco had the manners and bearing that the Corleonesi lacked. He had a large estate where he could entertain (and where, in the *grand guignol* of the Mafia war, opponents of Riina were invited for dinner and then murdered). Greco soon became known as "the pope"—not because of his power, which was largely illusory, but because he always carried holy cards in his pocket and quoted continually from the Bible.

All this would become clear later on. But in the murky world of the Mafia, where nothing is as it seems, it was far from clear while it was happening. Riina's forces first concentrated on consolidating their control of Catania, Agrigento and other provincial towns before turning their attention to Palermo. Here Stefano Bontate was still strong enough to resist. In fact, once he realized what was happening, he planned to kill Riina. When others urged him to consider the balance of power, Bontate, a handsome and arrogant man, said that he had two hundred soldiers to protect him and he was safe. But his loyalists had been picked off or had betrayed him. Riina had even gotten to Bontate's younger brother, playing on his jealousy and turning him into a spy.

On the evening of April 23, 1981, when he was leaving his forty-third birthday party, Bontate was gunned down at a stop sign, his Porsche speedster riddled with bullets. The Second Mafia War had officially broken out.

The three years that followed were the bloodiest in Palermo's history, marked by an endless chain of slaughter, mainly of members of the "losing families." Some murders were dramatic. Eight people were butchered in a stable that year, for instance, and when police finally arrived on the scene they found relatives trying to haul out the bodies before they arrived. But many more killings went unnoticed as *lupara bianca* disappearances. The total number of casualties of the Second Mafia War has never been ascertained. Some say they amounted to almost one thousand.

| | |

In their frenzy, the Corleonesi didn't limit themselves to hunting down "losing" Mafiosi.

On the morning of April 30, 1982, as the head of the Sicilian Communist Party, Pio La Torre, was driving to his party's headquarters in Palermo, he and his driver were attacked in a quiet, narrow street and shot repeatedly at close range. This time there was not a single assassin, but several of them using both a motorcycle and a car. They wanted to make sure of their work.

While the other illustrious corpses were those of local Sicilian figures—cops, judges, politicians—Pio La Torre had been a member of Parliament. Forced to take action, Rome dispatched a national hero to Palermo to direct the campaign against the Mafia.

General Carlo Alberto Dalla Chiesa was a *carabiniere* from head to foot, with all the bluff courtesy and charm of an old-time soldier—and with a soldier's will to victory. He had come up through the ranks and consolidated his legend by breaking the Red Brigades. Using a classical counterinsurgency approach, he had recruited an elite squad, then forced them to read the books of the Left and study the views of the Brigades; to learn to talk and think like them. A couple of his men had managed to infiltrate the organization and "turned" the first informer, a man named Pecci. When Pecci began to tell what he knew, it was a breakthrough, although it came at a great cost: the Brigades kidnapped his brother and videotaped his particularly gruesome interrogation and murder.

I always thought that by rights, Dalla Chiesa should have looked like the great Italian actor and director Vittorio De Sica: tall and elegant with a thin, handsome face and an Armani overcoat draped over his shoulders. In fact, the general was portly and round-faced, with shrewd eyes magnified by large glasses. His undistinguished looks were actually an advantage, helping him consistently to outfox the Red Brigades during the time they were bent on assassinating him. He would arrive at one event in his caravan of vehicles with full blaring sirens, and then, at the next, he would send his noisy official entourage while he himself walked up to the watching crowd and entered the event with everyone else.

The Red Brigades were desperate to get Dalla Chiesa, but they never did. He was far too wily. He never took the same route twice in a row. He would change his itinerary at the last minute, turn up where he was not expected, book one restaurant and go to another, travel by taxi one day and by bus another, never following a pattern.

Dalla Chiesa was a Piedmontese from Turin, but he was no stranger to Sicily. In the 1960s he had commanded the antibandit units of the *carabinieri*—ironically enough, in Corleone. He had been back since then, most notably in the 1970s, when Colonel Russo first picked up rumors that he might be a target of the Corleonesi. His prior experience having told him that Sicily was a land of "messages," Dalla Chiesa made a highly publicized trip to Corleone and spent an afternoon walking arm in arm with Russo on the city streets. The message was clear: if you hurt this man, you deal with me. Now he was getting a chance to make good on this promise.

We all believed that at last the Mafia would meet its match. We did not expect that Dalla Chiesa would never be given the special powers he had urgently requested, and did not know that there was scant enthusiasm for his appointment in the high reaches of the national government. It was rumored that years earlier, when he arrived at the building where Aldo Moro had been held, he found a copy of the "confession" that had been tortured out of Moro, and that this document contained damning information about some of the nation's leading politicians. Before leaving for Palermo, according to his diary, Dalla Chiesa had gone to see Giulio Andreotti, a seven-time premier and the dominant Italian politician of the postwar era. Andreotti was a cynical pragmatist who had a good claim to being a modern Machiavelli. (He had even coined Machiavellian aphorisms, such as "Power wears down those who do not possess it.") He was, moreover, excessively beholden to the votes delivered to the Christian Democrats by Sicily. Dalla Chiesa noted that when he told Andreotti he would look at everything—not just criminal activities, but political ties as well—Andreotti "went white." Soon afterward, Andreotti, who happened to be out of the government at that time, wrote an article wondering why Italy's leading military figure had to be sent to Sicily at all.

Despite the news that Dalla Chiesa had been enlisted in the struggle against the Mafia, I felt a growing unease about my own role. I had been elected to carry Piersanti Mattarella's banner of reform and rebirth, but instead of actively fighting for principle, I found myself ensnarled in the civic bureaucracy that even in the best of times, when the Mafia is not involved, paralyses Italian life. I seemed to spend my days wandering through the Palazzo delle Aquile trying to find a place where I could take hold and make an impact. Some days it was impossible even to summon indignation or react with passion to Palermo's daily horrors.

One evening I found myself sitting in a bar with my friend Raffaele Bonanni, who was also trying to breathe democratic life into the city, from the perspective of a union organizer.

"I've had it!" I finally exploded. "I'm going to resign and go back to my university work!"

"I've had it too," Raffaele echoed.

But then, as we talked further into the night, we convinced each other that Dalla Chiesa's appointment was a sign that Rome was serious about fighting the Mafia. By the time we saw the signs of first light outside, we had worked through our despair and pumped each other with new optimism.

Over the next few months, we began to make videos revealing the inefficiencies of the municipal government, the unfinished schools, the urban decay at the edges of Palermo and chaos in the historical center. After these videos were completed, we showed them on large screens in parish halls in various parts of the city. We demanded that the full city council be convened to discuss housing problems and urban decay in Palermo. Presenting ourselves as dissident Christian Democrats, we launched a petition drive protesting the inaction of the city government on these issues.

This work proceeded in association with an organization called "City of Man," formed by my old mentor, Father Pintacuda. That is what we wanted Palermo to be: a city of man, not a city of the Mafia. Pintacuda set out to organize strongly religious Catholics, convincing them to leave behind their resignation and *live* their Christianity through uncompromising political involvement. The City of Man became a crucial step in the civic renaissance that would eventually bloom in Palermo.

Dalla Chiesa went about his task unobtrusively, moving through town in a plain Fiat instead of the armored car he had been offered. But from the outset, the climate he worked in was hostile, petty, and obstructionist. The Mafia and its cultural and political assets saw to that. For instance, the general, for years a widower with three adult children, had a new wife, Emanuela, an attractive Red Cross nurse many years his junior. The relationship was soon the object of nasty gossip which was not so much gratuitous malice as a way of diminishing Dalla Chiesa's near-mythic stature.

I looked at the task he had inherited and saw exactly how daunting it was. The city he was trying to rehabilitate appeared to be living under an unofficial, self-imposed curfew. As soon as the shops closed, the streets would empty and people would hurry home. A claustral sense of dread and insecurity hung over Palermo like a pall, and even in the warm months, there was very little nightlife.

Socializing took place in people's homes, in cinemas or in restaurants. When the meal or film was over, there was no lingering in the streets or sitting at trattorias, none of that wonderful outdoor vivacity which renders the long, warm evenings of Mediterranean cities so charming.

Dalla Chiesa understood that one of the first things he had to do was give citizens a sense of security and a feeling that they had a right to their own city streets. And knowing that the Mafia spoke through "messages," he tried to create messages of equal eloquence for the antimafia that he—and some of us—hoped to inspire. Like us, he understood that a "military" response was not enough. The old general began to speak in schools; he met with businessmen and with the workers of Palermo; he spoke to the families of drug addicts and others in our bottomless social depths—always hoping to get them to affirm the importance of the rule of law. As he did all this, Palermo held its breath.

In one of the scenes in Giovanni Ferrara's movie *A Hundred Days in Palermo*, which tells the story of Dalla Chiesa in Sicily, the camera crew follows the general on a visit to the shipyards and shows one of the workers asking him, "What do you mean to do here, General? Cause a revolution?"

"A revolution?" Dalla Chiesa smiles. "No! I simply mean to apply the law."

The worker replies, "And wouldn't that be a revolution?"

| | |

In addition to using his reputation to reassure the people and urge them to greater civic consciousness, Dalla Chiesa slowly began to attack the Mafia at its roots. He served notice that he would go after the financial records that everyone knew could tell the whole story. ("The bankers have known very well for years who their Mafia clients are," he said.) For him, no subject and no individual was off limits. The day after the numerous offices of the Salvo cousins' empire were suddenly and thoroughly searched, the newspaper headlines read, "Dalla Chiesa in Action."

The general intended to uncover the rot from the top down. And he had no doubts about who was at the top; in his diary he wrote that the Andreotti faction was "in it up to their necks." But when he pressed Rome to grant him the special powers he required—getting access to inexplicably large bank accounts held by widows and common laborers, the power to tap suspects' telephones, and so on—he was met with obfuscation and delay. In his fight against the Red Brigades, he had all the resources he needed; but in Palermo he was isolated, lacking even the elite force of men he had previously counted on to back him up.

He saw what was happening: "The Mafia and I are studying each other as in a chess game. The Mafia is cautious, slow. It takes your measure, listens to you, checks you from a distance."

In the meantime, the bodies created by the Mafia War continued to multiply—at one point, ten corpses in five days from what became known as the "triangle of death," three small towns just beyond Palermo; then two bodies dumped a few meters from a *carabinieri* barracks; then an execution in Palermo's central Vucciria market; the murder of a Mafioso of the Corleonesi along with the three *carabinieri* and driver transporting him to Rome for prosecution, all massacred on the way to the airport. After this last event, there was a phone call to police headquarters, with a muffled voice declaring ominously that "Operation Carlo Alberto is almost concluded."

Dalla Chiesa was spooked. On September 2 he went to the United States Consulate and pleaded with the Americans to lean on the authorities in Rome to force them to give him the assistance he needed.

The next night I was at home when the phone rang. I picked it up and listened in disbelief as an agitated friend gasped: "They've killed him!"

"Killed whom?" I held my breath.

"Dalla Chiesa!"

The general had been struck with a hail of Kalashnikov fire in his car, and with him, his young wife Emanuela, whose body he had tried to shield as he was dying. The next day, on the wall of a building in central Via Carini where the attack had occurred, an anonymous citizen hung a sheet of paper scribbled with these words: HERE DIES THE HOPE OF HONEST PALERMITANS.

| | |

The bodies of Dalla Chiesa and his wife lay in state in Villa Whitaker, the Prefecture of Palermo. During the vigil I met for the first time Nando, Rita and Simona Dalla Chiesa, the general's son and daughters by his first marriage, all of whom were to become very close to me in the years ahead. Then, as the authorities of Italy, including the president of the Republic and the prime minister, converged on Palermo, I flew out of Punta Raisi Airport to give a long-scheduled speech at a conference in Viareggio, a seaside resort in Tuscany. I was relieved not to have to watch the crocodile tears of those politicians who had snubbed and isolated Dalla Chiesa, and blocked him from the means that would have saved his life and allowed him to fulfill his mission.

But the funeral turned out to be a momentous occasion. Outside the Church of San Domenico, a large, Spanish-baroque basilica in the center of the city, tens of thousands of people, ordinary citizens of all callings and social classes, crowded the square. And as the official cars of the authorities began to pull up, the people, instead of obediently making way for the dignitaries, contemptuously showered them with 100 lire coins (worth only a few pennies even then). The message was clear enough: "You've been bought—but you're worth so little!" The politicians hustled into the church as the people spat and yelled abuse. But once inside, they were confronted with Nando, Rita and Simona Dalla Chiesa standing in mute sorrow beside their father's casket. That morning they had indignantly refused the wreath sent by the president of the Sicilian Region. Now they scornfully ignored the condolences offered them by the officials from Rome. The only one they embraced was the president of the Republic, Sandro Pertini.

The Mass was said by Cardinal Archbishop Pappalardo, himself son of a Sicilian *carabiniere*, who also pointedly ignored all the authorities present except President Pertini. In a chilling moment—for the church and for Sicily—he began his homily: "There is a famous phrase from Latin literature, Sallust, I believe, that comes to mind: *Dum Romae consulitur… Saguntum expugnatur.* While Rome considers what is to be done, the city of Saguntum is sacked. But this time it is not Saguntum, it is Palermo! Our poor Palermo!"

It was an incandescent moment. An unequivocal statement about who was responsible for our tragedy coming from a prince of the Church, which itself for decades had at best been *omertosa* (a passive mental state of *omertà*, or silence) about the Mafia.

Everyone present got the message. This murder had not just happened; it had been *allowed* to happen; it was a predictable result of the regime that had taken over our lives. The Mafia was what it was because it lay *within*—in the state, the Church, the culture. The corollary was clear, too: the only way to beat the Mafia was to *throw it out*—out of the state, the Church, the culture; out of civil society.

With the cardinal's words, another tenuous step toward the civic renewal of Palermo had been taken. As with other steps, we could not discern this at the time, yet Pappalardo had begun to expel the Mafia from our hearts. The impact was different only in scale from that of the Pope's thundering denunciations of the Communist empire in Eastern Europe, occurring at the same time.

When I returned from Viareggio, I found a city still reeling under the shock of Dalla Chiesa's death and the force of Cardinal Pappalardo's words. Some newspapers were reporting the visit that the general had made to the American consul in Palermo the day before, to plead for the United States government to intervene and keep him from being isolated. But it was too late. His time had already run out.

It took Dalla Chiesa's death and the outrage that followed for the Italian Parliament to finally remember, discuss and pass the bill that Pio La Torre had introduced before he was murdered. Despite its hard provisions—making an "association of a Mafia type" itself a crime; and creating provision for the tracing, freezing and confiscation of Mafia assets—the bill quickly became the Rognoni–La Torre Law, the current minister of the interior joining his name to La Torre's. Still, those who were outraged at the general's murder were not appeased, nor did they turn their gaze away from the political world. Nando Dalla Chiesa gave an interview to the national newspaper *La Repubblica* in which he baldly stated: "I think that [my father's assassination] was a political crime, both decided and committed in Palermo. Neither I nor others of my family are interested in knowing who the killers were…. We are interested that the instigators be identified and punished and, in my opinion, they must be looked for within the Sicilian Christian Democratic Party."

| | |

In a few weeks, Pope John Paul II made his first visit to Palermo. After Cardinal Pappalardo's words at the Dalla Chiesa funeral, there was particularly great anticipation on the part of all Palermo's citizens, Catholics and non-Catholics, that the Holy Father would officially excommunicate members of the Mafia. In fact, the embargoed copies of his speech distributed to journalists contained a very tough paragraph against Cosa Nostra. But this section was no longer in the text that the Pope read. Eleven years were to elapse before John Paul II returned to Sicily and lifted his voice in an unforgettable accusation of the "Men of the Mafia."

A lesson we had by now assimilated was that he who is isolated is killed—and now we feared for our cardinal. Several of us immediately decided to write a book that we called *One Voice, One City*, each of us contributing an article with a common theme: Cardinal Pappalardo was not saying anything particularly new, and we *all* shared his views. We hoped to make it clear—to the Church as well as to the Mafia—that the cardinal was not alone, and that many concerned Catholics stood not behind, but right beside him.

As I look back on those events today, I must honestly admit that if I didn't lose my faith, I owe it to Cardinal Pappalardo—and of course to God. Pappalardo showed us all that faith and legality are inseparable, at a time when many of the most influential figures in our society were maintaining that law belongs to Caesar and faith to God. When previous cardinals had said that the Mafia did not exist, and acted accordingly, they in effect encouraged the parish priest of any small village to curry favor with the local *capomafia* for the honor of being allowed to perform the marriage ceremony of his son or daughter, or baptize his children and grandchildren, or officiate at his funeral. But when the head of the Sicilian Church says that the Mafia is evil and Mafiosi are sinners, that same parish priest will think twice before ignoring the Mafia connections of his parishioners. What Cardinal Pappalardo did was bring Catholics openly opposed to the Mafia, who once were pushed to the back pews of the church, directly up to the altar and show them a sign of grace.

I wish I could say that the cardinal's courage was recognized and rewarded, but this was not the case. On Easter 1983, he decided to celebrate Mass in the chapel of Ucciardone, Palermo's nineteenth-century prison, built at the time of the Kingdom of the Two Sicilies. Looking very much like a fortress, it stands close to the city's waterfront and is primarily inhabited by Mafiosi. Going to Ucciardone was Pappalardo's way of saying to these low-level soldiers, "I'm against the Mafia, but I'm your pastor, and my heart and ministry are open to receive you." When he arrived at the prison, however, the director of the prison told him with great embarrassment that not a single prisoner had come to the chapel. This despite the fact that it was Easter, and even on ordinary Sundays the chapel was always filled with Mafiosi who found no contradiction in thinking of themselves as devout Catholics. The Mafia had sent its message in reply to Cardinal Pappalardo's denunciations. So the cardinal said his Mass in front of the director and a handful of prison guards.

What happened at Ucciardone was not only an insult but an unequivocal threat, and newspapers all over the country carried the news with loud headlines. Afterward, Pappalardo was offered body-guards by the national Committee for Security, but he declined. He continued to speak with authority, but never again with his former openness and passion—not because of personal fear, but rather (it was said) because of orders from the Vatican. Still, the cardinal had shown the way. And now it was for us who lived in the world of Caesar to do our part to bring God there.

CHAPTER

5

I love elephants. I think of them as clumsy yet gentle animals, creatures of a distant past who have stayed around to keep us company. My love for these big, ungainly inhabitants of faraway lands has led me to collect them in all sizes and forms. My collection now numbers a few hundred: glass elephants, wooden elephants, elephant bells, elephant book ends, African elephants and their Indian cousins. Some are very beautiful, some kitsch, but I love them all; and whenever I add a new one to my collection, I feel a childlike joy. Milli says that one day we will move out and let the elephants have the whole house instead of just part of it.

Rocco Chinnici was to me an elephant, in form and in spirit. He was a big, slouching, rumpled man, rough and refined at the same time, with a loud trumpeting voice and an excellent memory. This last quality was a distinct asset for the head of the Investigating Magistrates' Office in Palermo. Yet Chinnici did not want to rely on himself or any other single individual to know everything about a given case. He had imported into Sicily the concept of a prosecution team or "pool" to help combat the Mafia. This innovation had arisen on the Italian mainland in the 1970s during the fight against terrorism. It made for better teamwork among prosecutors, and more importantly, it kept any one of them from being the sole repository of knowledge about a given case, which could therefore be obliterated by assassination.

I had first met Chinnici right after Piersanti Mattarella's murder, when he had interviewed me in hopes of turning up information about the killers. I went to Chinnici's office and told him frankly how Piersanti had thwarted the interests of Ciancimino and the Salvos, which was tantamount to thwarting the interests of their colleagues in the Mafia. When we had finished talking, Chinnici took my arm and accompanied me to the door. "You know the difference between you and me?" he asked. "Even though we think exactly the same things, you as a politician can say them without having to prove them, but to put these same accusations into an indictment, I must have proof."

Chinnici and I had kept in touch after this, sometimes going with Father Pintacuda to speak to schoolchildren about the Mafia. Young people already knew the war stories. Rocco Chinnici considered it important to tell them how the Mafiosi affected their lives and defined their world.

The newspapers had for some time been writing about an investigation the police had been pursuing. It was called "The Report of the 162," but a more accurate title would have been "The Report of the 161 plus Michele Greco," because the focus was on the man Totò Riina had installed as head of the Commission. When the report was handed over to Chinnici, journalists hinted that something "big" was in the offing. They spoke of a particular magistrate in Chinnici's office, a man named Giovanni Falcone—alleged to be a whiz at following money trails and other investigative techniques—who was working on the case along with a colleague. Then at the beginning of July 1983, Falcone signed warrants for the arrest of fourteen major Mafiosi accused of being involved in Dalla Chiesa's assassination. Among them were names soon to become world famous: Greco, Riina, Bernardo Provenzano—all heads of the Corleonesi.

On the morning of July 29, another in a string of clear, hot, cloudless days, Rocco Chinnici greeted the concierge who was standing just outside his apartment building in Via Pipitone Federico. A pair of his *carabinieri* bodyguards were there. His driver had the armored car idling and his two escort cars had the side streets blocked until the motorcade could depart. Suddenly there was a huge blast that rattled windows a mile away. Pieces of metal flew into the air and windows all over the neighborhood collapsed in cascades of glass. The mangled pieces of four bodies were scattered for hundreds of meters—Rocco Chinnici, his two bodyguards and the hapless concierge. (The driver was miraculously saved by the car.) This was the first time the Mafia had used a remote-controlled car bomb—the Semtex explosive had been purchased from a Lebanese arms dealer. The next day's papers ran their stories under the headline "Palermo Like Beirut."

| | |

The following months were marked by a brief effort on the part of the Christian Democrats to clean up their image; and then, as time passed after Chinnici's illustrious corpse was given a state funeral and buried, they slowly returned to their old ways.

I was in my office when, somewhat to my amazement, in came Giuseppe Insalaco, the "tainted" city councilor who had insisted on acknowledging the Mafia's existence. As usual, the short, stocky man was talking nonstop, beginning even before I asked him to take a seat: "Look, there's a possibility that I'm going to be voted in as mayor. It's the dream of my life to be mayor of Palermo, but if you're standing as candidate, I'll withdraw. I don't stand a chance against you; I'm just Peppuccio Insalaco… you're *Professor* Orlando."

I immediately assured him that I wouldn't think of standing in his way, not at this point in our city's history.

At that time, the mayor was not directly elected by the people, but chosen by a majority of city council members. And "Peppuccio," as Insalaco kept calling himself in our conversation, was indeed chosen. The vote took place in the basement of the building that housed the Christian Democrat headquarters (this in itself was both ironic and symbolic), and when the result was tallied, it was unanimous except for one blank ballot—mine.

"Thank you, my dear colleagues," said Insalaco "because with the exception of my own vote, you have all given me your vote of confidence."

The next day I walked into the mayor's office and Insalaco came toward me, his eyes feverish in his dark, square face: "And now they're gonna see who Peppuccio Insalaco is! They'll see if I'm just a lackey or the mayor of Palermo!"

I didn't need to ask who "they" were.

His eyes fixed on my face, Insalaco continued: "First thing, I'm gonna drown Palermo in posters in memory of the second anniversary of Pio La Torre's death! So much for Ciancimino!"

His use of Ciancimino's name was interesting. Salvo Lima, whose name was associated with Ciancimino's in the public mind, had been linked to the Bontate-Badalamenti faction, while Ciancimino, coming from Corleone, was tied to the Corleonesi. Until 1979 it was Lima who was at the top, being a member of Parliament in Rome as well as a local politician. Then Lima, perhaps sensing the wind beginning to blow from Corleone, ran for and was elected to the European Parliament, thus receding from a direct role in Palermo's politics, where Ciancimino was now up and Lima down.

Over the next few months, Insalaco went about the business of being mayor as if bent on ransoming his past. Why did he do it? Did he, who also had always been linked to the Bontate-Badalamenti losing faction, fear the Corleonesi? Did he want to look his children in the face? Whatever the answer, Insalaco knew where the bodies were buried, and we wondered if he would actually go so far as to begin digging.

For thirty-five years the contracts for the upkeep of streets and sewers and for street lighting had been automatically renewed to the same company in defiance of the municipal law requiring public bids. Not surprisingly, the cost for the illumination of Palermo's streets was almost three times that of Milan or Turin, much larger cities. Nor was it surprising that the streets and sewers were in appalling condition, although maintaining them cost far more than in any other Italian city of comparable size. Insalaco broke with the past and called for open bids. The hostility he faced was immediate and severe, led by the lawyers of the companies that had always gotten the contracts. Insalaco had to watch some of his commissioners openly telephoning Ciancimino for orders on how to vote—in the city government chambers, in view of him and everybody else, without the slightest embarrassment or shame.

Mayor Insalaco decided to name a central street of the city after Carlo Alberto Dalla Chiesa. On the day the new name was unveiled, before all the authorities, many of them Mafia people, he said: "With Peppuccio Insalaco as mayor, a street is named after General Carlo Alberto Dalla Chiesa. With Ciancimino as mayor, the street would have been named after Luciano Leggio." As he spoke these words, there was a collective intake of breath.

In July 1984, I was in one of the suburban districts for an official ceremony representing Insalaco, who was elsewhere engaged. He arrived unexpectedly and sat down beside me, whispering feverishly: "I can't take it! I can't take it any more! They're going to kill me! Understand? If I don't resign they're going to kill me! I tried... but now I've got to give up. Only you can be mayor of Palermo. If you call Rome, someone will answer. If I call Rome, the phone is always busy."

I could tell that he was terrified. His hands were shaking. His eyes darted around to spot the potential gunman in our midst. He confessed that he had sent his daughter to London to keep her out of harm's way. Not long after, Insalaco resigned. In the square in front of Palazzo delle Aquile, near where I was standing, I heard one of Ciancimino's men say to another: "That *infame!* He thinks he is a moralizer...!"

In the culture of the Mafia, *infame* does not mean "infamous." The word is used in Sicilian to indicate a traitor, and it bears a connotation of contempt and hatred, and possible vengeance. A few days later, Insalaco was accused of having once embezzled some funds belonging to a charity. The charge was perfectly plausible and probably true—I wouldn't have put it past him—but it was clear that Ciancimino, not the criminal justice system, was behind this revelation.

| | |

With the Insalaco debacle, the Christian Democratic Party was in a mess. A commissioner was sent by the party in Rome to take the situation into his hands. He informed me that Rome had decided that I was to be mayor, to which I immediately replied that the current political environment of Palermo made this impossible. He kept insisting and I kept refusing, in a tug of war that went on for several days.

I sought advice from others. First I saw an old Communist friend, Michele Figurelli, who flatly told me that if I accepted, I would be the mayor of Lima and Ciancimino's Christian Democracy and that his own party would oppose me with all their might. Then I saw my Catholic friends from City of Man, and their pitying looks and shrugging shoulders said more than any words. Then I sought out Father Pintacuda, who as always was submerged in chaotic piles of books, press clippings and magazines. As I described the offer, his face was enigmatic, almost expressionless, but his eyes bored through me: "If you accept, you'll be committing a serious mistake." And then, after we had discussed the possibilities further, he added: "And if you do it, you'll have me as a strenuous opponent."

Exhausted, half-drunk from having drained, glass after glass, a bottle of Amaro Averna—a Sicilian bitter herbal drink, the only refreshment he had to offer me—I turned to take my leave.

"Luca, don't despair," he said, once more becoming my spiritual advisor. "Read St. Paul's letter to the Romans."

When I got home, it was almost two o'clock in the morning and Milli and the girls were asleep. I found a Bible and read the book of Romans. It contains so much hope and so many cautions. I fell asleep wondering which particular passage Father Pintacuda had

had in mind. But I woke up the next day resolved to ignore all the advice I had solicited and take the plunge.

That evening, in the Christian Democrat headquarters, there was long applause, shouts of "Orlando for Mayor" and sweaty outstretched hands grasping mine in enthusiasm. I suddenly yelled: "Just a minute! Just a minute! I want my designation to be put to the vote… not by unanimous agreement but by secret ballots!"

The mood turned to consternation and people looked at each other uncertainly.

"Either a secret ballot or I don't take the job," I kept repeating.

Finally there was a ballot and I received seven votes out of forty-one Christian Democrat councilors present. Afterward I treated myself to a pizza in magnificent solitude in the only pizzeria open at that time of night. I felt as if a huge weight had fallen from my shoulders.

I later learned that around the time I was eating, Vito Ciancimino was commenting on what had happened: "Who does he think he is? Does he think he can become mayor of Palermo without even giving me a phone call?"

The next day I paid Father Pintacuda another visit. The three telephones on his desk were ringing incessantly and for once his face was beaming.

"Yes, they voted against him!" he was yelling happily into the receiver. "Yes, it was seven votes out of forty-one! A great victory! A great victory!"

| | |

That summer of 1984, the summer of my not being chosen mayor, the criminal justice system was finally beginning a coordinated move against the Mafia, and the events it set in motion would offer definitive insights into what kind of organization we were dealing with. The impenetrable wall of *omertà* had not only cracked, but split wide open. Tommaso Buscetta, a Mafioso known as "the boss of two worlds" because of his activities on both sides of the Atlantic, had started talking. And once he had started, he didn't stop.

Precisely speaking, Buscetta was only a "soldier" in the rigidly hierarchical Mafia structure. He never became a capo because of an untidy personal life—he had left his first wife, taken a mistress with whom he had two children, and then married another woman—which the Mafia, strangely puritanical about such things, frowned upon. Yet he was a man of such abilities that his role had never been that of just another *picciotto*. He had the personality and presence of a boss, and over the years had become a charismatic and commanding figure in Cosa Nostra, acquiring an international reputation.

Buscetta got his start during the First Mafia War, and in the crackdown that followed made his way to the United States, where he helped to solidify the links between the Sicilian and the American branches of Cosa Nostra until his arrest and expulsion from the country. Still wanted in Italy, Buscetta next went to Brazil, where he lived like a grandee until his arrest for drug trafficking in 1972 and deportation back to Italy. After a jail term, he was paroled in 1980 and immediately fled to Brazil again—as before, keeping in touch and involved from his large ranch. As the Second Mafia War broke out, Gaetano Badalamenti had tried to persuade Buscetta to return to Sicily and restore peace. But Buscetta saw from afar what even those who were on the ground did not: that the Corleonesi coup was virtually complete. Although he refused to become involved in the conflict, Buscetta was presumed by the Corleonesi to be sympathetic to their enemies, and so his son, son-in-law, brother, nephew, and a dozen other relatives were all killed. When he was arrested again by Brazilian authorities, Buscetta finally agreed to open the Mafia's inner sanctum.

Buscetta would ultimately become a media celebrity in Italy as well as an example of defiance that would encourage Salvatore Contorno, Antonio Calderone, and eventually—as the fight against the Mafia started to be won—a flood of other *pentiti* ("penitents") to come forward, breaking the code of *omertà* and adding one by one to the picture of an evil state within the state. With his mestizo features, pomaded hair and pencil mustache, Buscetta looked like central casting's idea of the Mafioso. He imperiously rejected the term *pentito* when the Italian press coined it to describe him. He was a man of honor and had done nothing to repent, he said, and was talking about the Mafia only because its principles had been compromised from within by a violent and amoral cult of "crazies." He insisted on the "morality" of the "old Mafia" these interlopers had conquered. In a perfect expression of what amounted to the Mafia's foundation myth, Buscetta told government interrogators about a turn-of-the-century Sicilian romance his father had read to him when he was growing up. Called *Beati Paoli*, the book tells of a poor orphan whose mother, an aristocrat, is killed by a relative of hers who controls society. The child is brought up in the back streets of Palermo by a secret cult named the Beati Paoli, whose members live in the catacombs of the city, emerging periodically to exact revenge and do justice in the corrupt world above. (Today there is a Piazza Beati Paoli in Palermo at the spot where, tradition holds, the entry to the underground once stood.) The Beati Paoli, said Buscetta, were what the Mafia had been before it was betrayed from within.

Tommaso Buscetta was actually not the first informer. In 1973, a Mafioso named Leonardo Vitale had undergone a spiritual crisis and turned himself in. He told police about Leggio and Riina and Vito Ciancimino. He admitted having committed murders and gave specifics. But because he framed his confessions in terms of his religious rebirth, he was not believed. In fact, he was declared insane and sent to a criminal asylum.

Five years later, in 1978, Giuseppe Di Cristina—a boss, not a soldier like Vitale—made his confessions to the *carabinieri*. He too was ignored at the time, although the chilling and detailed picture he painted of the Corleonesi was resurrected later on when this faction began its inexorable move to power and when Buscetta arrived on the scene.

Buscetta was different from the other two informers. He knew all the secrets and had dealt for years with the other bosses on an equal footing. He was able to explain everything—rules, traditions, businesses, narcotics—with incredible detail. He described the organization from the inside out, laying out the hierarchy that linked the soldiers in the street to the top bosses in the Commission. He was living history, his memories going back to 1963 when the American Mafiosi, under pressure at home because of the revelations of Joseph Valachi, had convened a meeting with Sicilian counterparts at the Hotel delle Palme in Palermo, and convinced them to modernize and take on a twentieth-century persona. Now Buscetta was becoming the Valachi of Sicily.

| | |

The fact that a highly placed Mafioso was talking to investigators was kept secret for over two months. Then, on September 29, 1984, the newsrooms across Italy were hit by a bombshell: 366 warrants had been issued for the arrest of major Mafiosi, and most of them were already in custody as a result of a midnight sweep by police forces. Sirens screeched all day in Palermo as police vans slashed through the streets, transporting the arrested to jails all over the country—but not to the Ucciardone, where the Mafia reigned supreme. At one point during the night, the police ran out of handcuffs.

More amazing even than the arrests of hundreds of killers and drug traffickers, a few weeks later "Don" Vito Ciancimino was arrested and had a mug shot taken. At this point he collapsed and had to be practically carried out to the car waiting to take him to prison. Only ten days later, the all-powerful Salvo cousins, Nino and Ignazio, went the same way.

My reaction to these arrests was like that of most Palermo citizens: wonderment and satisfaction, and a guarded optimism about the possibility that real change might actually be accomplished.

There were to be elections in the following spring, and the

national secretary of the Christian Democratic Party, a man called Ciriaco De Mita, bravely decided that drastic action finally had to be taken. The idea that Ciancimino had been arrested, not just for having an affinity to the Mafia but for being a sworn member, hung heavily over the party. In an effort to give a veneer of legitimacy to the Sicilian Christian Democrats, Piersanti Mattarella's brother Sergio was named commissioner for Palermo, and he asked me to be his deputy.

Because of the approaching elections, the first thing that needed to be done was to clean up the Christian Democratic list. We began scrutinizing each potential candidate, using information obtained from investigators. It fell to me to have to inform those who were no longer to stand as candidates that the party had decided they were out. One ex-commissioner, a protégé of Ciancimino, wept pitifully, swearing that he was honest, had never personally stolen anything, and had a family to keep. Another listened in stony silence and then snarled at me: "How many children have you got?"

As the campaign got under way, De Mita traveled between Rome and Palermo more and more frequently. He was fearful during his time in the city, and every time he left he would call home from the car phone: "I'm leaving Palermo now." I could almost hear the implied sequel: *and I'm still in one piece.* The fact that he expressed his fears only about the city of Palermo, as if the rest of the island were immune from the Mafia, irritated me intensely. So I deliberately tormented him in the hope that he might begin to understand the reality in which we lived and operated every day of our lives. Once we were driving to Termini Imerese, a small town east of Palermo, and he made his usual phone call as we left the city behind. I said nothing until we arrived in Termini. Getting out of the car, I pointed at some pedestrian and whispered: "See that man with the beard? He's well known as a bloodthirsty Mafioso."

De Mita blanched. "What, here in Termini as well?"

"Do you think the Mafia stops at Palermo? And can you see that other guy coming toward us? Watch it! If you're seen walking with him, your political career is finished!"

The Christian Democrats' national secretary spent the whole day fearfully looking over his shoulder. My taunt had hit the mark.

My parents, Salvatore Orlando
and Eleonora Cammarata, on
their wedding day.

ABOVE: My mother arranges my hair for my first Holy Communion in 1954.

RIGHT: This was taken of me in 1957 when I was at Gonzaga, forced to wear the dreaded smock.

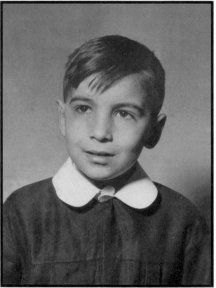

ABOVE: Milli and I spent our honeymoon in Mexico in 1971.

BELOW: Our daughters, Leila and Eleonora, were 4 and 8 years old when this photo was taken in 1982.

LEFT: Piersanti Mattarella was one of the most influential figures in my life, a man who showed me that it was possible, even in my devastated country, for politics to be an honorable profession.

BELOW: In 1985, I was elected mayor of Palermo for the first time by the city council.

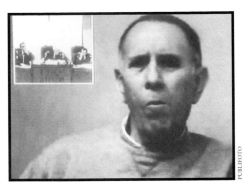

ABOVE LEFT: Stefano Bontate was on the losing side of the Second Mafia War, a victim of the Corleonesi.

ABOVE RIGHT: Unlike Bontate, Gaetano Badalamenti saw how powerful the Corleonesi had become and managed to survive the Second Mafia War.

BELOW: Cesare Terranova (left) and Pio La Torre (right) were among the first of the illustrious corpses produced by the Corleonesi.

ABOVE: General Carlo Alberto Dalla Chiesa, an Italian hero.

RIGHT: Tommaso Buscetta during a Mafia trial in 1972. His face would change after he became a *pentito* and was given plastic surgery.

BELOW: Giovanni Falcone (left) and Paolo Borsellino.

ABOVE: Falcone and I share a
moment during the long struggle
against the Mafia.

BELOW: I was privileged to receive
Communion from Cardinal
Salvatore Pappalardo, who spoke
out against Mafia criminality at a
crucial moment in our history.

PUBLIFOTO

ABOVE: I joined my friend and mentor, Father Ennio Pintacuda, in a torchlight procession in memory of Father Puglisi after he was murdered in 1994.

BELOW: The opening of the Maxitrial in the "Bunker Courtroom" in 1986.

PUBLIFOTO

RIGHT: Vito Ciancimino after his arrest.

BELOW: Totò Riina in the Bunker Courtroom.

ABOVE: Giulio Andreotti (left) and Salvo Lima shortly before Lima's murder.

BELOW: In 1988, Milli (third from left) and I were forced to seek asylum in Soviet Georgia.

ABOVE: May 23, 1992, a day of infamy. This was the scene after a bomb blast near the Punta Raisi Airport killed Giovanni Falcone and his wife, Francesca, along with three bodyguards.

BELOW: Two months later, on July 20, another bomb blast on Via D'Amelio in Palermo killed Paolo Borsellino and five bodyguards.

ABOVE: Wherever I went, I was surrounded by bodyguards of my own.

BELOW: In 1992 I campaigned for the Italian Parliament.

ABOVE: In La Rete's headquarters during the campaign, people such as the famous photographer Letizia Battaglia (right) joined in the fight.

RIGHT: The antimafia movement spread from Palermo to the rest of Italy. Here I address a meeting in Bologna.

BELOW: In December 1997, I took office at the city hall after my election as mayor.

SHOBHA

ABOVE: The Teatro Massimo during restoration.

BELOW: The Massimo on the long-awaited day of its reopening.

PUBLIFOTO

ABOVE: Paolo Borsellino's widow, Rita, joined me in granting a "certificate of adoption" of a public monument to pupils taking part in the Palermo Renaissance.

BELOW: In June 1999, Hillary Clinton and I were welcomed at Santa Maria dello Spasimo by students participating in the "Adopt a Monument" program.

ABOVE: These junior high school students "adopted" St. Peter's Bastion in the Palermo Royal Palace.

BELOW: Another landmark moment in the rebirth of Palermo was the signing conference for the United Nations Convention Against Transnational Organized Crime on December 14, 2000, at the Zisa Cultural Center. From left to right: Adolph Hirschfeld, of the Directorate of Corruption and Economic Crime, Botswana; Mayor Orlando; Roy Godson, Professor of Government, Georgetown University; Lorenzo Gomez Morin, Minister of Education, Baja California, Mexico; Alan Lai, of the Independent Commission Against Corruption, Hong Kong.

6

July 28, 1985, was my last day as a free man. It was the last day that I walked the streets by myself, the last day that I went down to the newspaper stand to buy a newspaper, the last day that I casually dropped into an espresso bar to enjoy a cup of coffee. It was the last day I ever drove a car. Today my driver's license has expired. The bulletproof Alfa Romeo of 1985 has been replaced by an armor-plated Lancia. And my escort, then an elderly civilian driver and a municipal policeman, has now grown to several specially trained police bodyguards. Wherever I go now, even when I am abroad, there is often a lead car in front and a car following.

The Christian Democrats lost ten seats in the 1985 municipal elections, but the party still had a majority in the newly elected council. The primary reason the caucus chose me as mayor was that it realized it had to produce a new look. It had to appear to be breaking with a soiled past, not only because the voters were becoming disaffected but also because there was a massive Mafia trial looming up ahead and some of the old party supporters were going to be defendants.

That same July 28, my last day of freedom, was the last day on this earth for a smart, courageous policeman named Beppe Montana. Beppe loved the sea and boats and he had just spent a carefree day with his fiancée and some friends out in his motorboat, cruising along the bays and inlets east of Palermo. They had returned to Porticello, a small fishing village where he kept his boat, when, still wearing his T-shirt and clogs, he was shot and killed. Another terrible Palermo summer had begun.

Beppe Montana, who was head of a section of the special squad called *Catturandi* (from the word for "capture"), was responsible for hunting down the many Mafiosi who were wanted and on the run. He had already made several important arrests. And after his death, it emerged that the Sunday outing when he was killed may not have been entirely for recreational purposes. He suspected that some of the villas along that stretch of coastline might shelter fugitive Mafiosi, and he was probably trying to get a closer look at what was going on. That would have given the Mafia an extra incentive to get rid of him.

My first day as mayor was therefore marked by blood—old blood and newly spilt blood. In the morning, the second anniversary of Rocco Chinnici's death, I went to lay a wreath in front of the house on Via Pepitone Federico where he had been blown up. In the afternoon I was at a small church in Santa Flavia, nearby Porticello, for a Requiem Mass in memory of Beppe Montana.

Montana had not been alone when he was killed. One of the people with him was able to describe a car and remember the first numbers of the license plate. Having traced the car, the police hauled in a young man, Salvatore Marino, in whose run-down house they found the huge sum of 34 million lire in cash wrapped up in a newspaper bearing the date of July 28, the day the hit took place. What exactly happened at the police department the night Marino was brought in has never been ascertained. What is certain is that the next day he was dead, his body swollen and disfigured from beatings.

In my first week as mayor, therefore, the legal system which I was committed not only to uphold but to strengthen made a tragic error that appalled the partisans of democracy and gave the political representatives of the underworld an opportunity to blast the police and prosecutors. The coffin of Salvatore Marino—not Beppe Montana, the man he had murdered—was carried through the city as that of a martyred hero. As I watched it pass by, I got a sense of what lay ahead for me when I heard a few cries of "Long live the Mafia!"

The tension in the city was as heavy as the summer humidity. Police headquarters was torn by recriminations. Italy's minister of the interior, Oscar Luigi Scalfaro, ordered that the head of the special squad and two others be removed. Against this backdrop I presented my program to the city council.

The afternoon of the following day—siesta time in Palermo—I was in my office, working alone. In a few hours, the council would debate my proposals to improve life in our city. Except for my driver and bodyguard and a few sleepy municipal employees, there was nobody around. The phone rang. It was a reporter with the newspaper *L'Ora*. His voice broke as he spoke.

"They've killed Ninni Cassarà."

I couldn't believe what I was being told. It wouldn't register. Then I heard the familiar screams of sirens heading toward Viale Croce Rossa, where my friend Ninni, Palermo's deputy chief of police, lived.

When I got there, I saw his body on the first steps of the stairs in a pool of blood. He had managed to drag himself inside the entrance, but had been hit by so many bullets that he bled to death. Near him was the body of another policeman, Roberto Antiochia, in his early twenties, who had been on leave in Rome when he heard of Beppe Montana's death and returned immediately to Palermo, demanding to go back to work as Ninni Cassarà's bodyguard. A hit squad of at least fifteen people was waiting for them when they got out of their cars and approached Ninni's flat. More than two hundred Kalashnikov shell casings were found on the street. A third policeman, Natale Mondo, was sitting on the edge of a flower bed, looking like death. He rose, broke into sobs, and embraced me. He held me, his whole body shaking.

I suddenly began to yell: "Basta! Basta! Basta!" It was the desperation and anger of a citizen, as well as the mayor of a city at war. It was also the desperation and anger of a friend.

Ninni and I had been in many of the same classes at the university. He loved playing cards and tennis, and he did his work with intelligence and passion. I had last seen him at Beppe Montana's funeral, but the last time we had had a chance to talk at length had been about a month before that, when I ran into him on the street. I was headed toward my house and Ninni was coming out of a shop with a pack of cigarettes in his hand.

"How are things?" I asked him.

"Not so good, Luca. Not too good at all. Actually, one of these days I'd like to talk to you and tell you how bad things are."

He never got a chance to tell me exactly what he meant, but how bad things were was proven by Ninni's body sprawled out in his hallway, covered in blood.

It emerged that he had been working nonstop for days, not even going home to eat or sleep, trying to deal with the Montana murder and the events surrounding the death of Salvatore Marino. Then, after so many days of living at his office, Ninni had suddenly called his wife, Laura, to tell her that he was coming home for a late lunch. How did the killers know he was going home? Was his telephone tapped? The press began to speak openly of a Mafia mole within the police forces.

I returned to Palazzo delle Aquile and called Rino Nicolosi, president of the Region, for an emergency meeting. It was early evening when I arrived at his office—once the office of Piersanti Mattarella—yet I insisted that he call the prime minister and the minister of the interior in Rome. We could not be left alone: that had to be our message. But the prime minister, Bettino Craxi, was reportedly too busy to talk with Nicolosi, and so was the minister of the interior, Oscar Luigi Scalfaro. Furious, I grabbed the phone and demanded to speak to the prime minister. When he came on the line, I insisted that a Sicilian delegation must meet with him immediately. After hesitating for a moment, he agreed.

We left on a special flight the next morning and were waiting at the prime minister's office when he arrived. He offered to come to Palermo, along with Scalfaro and Francesco Cossiga, the president of the Republic. I said we were grateful, but after the meeting I took Scalfaro aside for a conversation. I didn't really know him yet, although in time I would come to appreciate his firm sense of principle. But for now, because of the disarray of law enforcement in Palermo, I had to broach a difficult issue.

"Mr. Minister," I stammered, not wanting to get into the details of the dissension among our law enforcement officials, "perhaps it might be wise if you didn't come to Palermo right now."

Scalfaro's response taught me something. "A minister of the interior goes where he is applauded," he said. "But he must be equally prepared to accept insults."

And so we all returned for yet another state funeral in Palermo's magnificent cathedral. Laura Cassarà, Ninni's widow, had insisted on commemorating his death privately. So this was Roberto Antiochia's funeral, although everyone was treating it as Ninni's too. The cathedral was packed. This time the anger welled up not from ordinary citizens, as in the case of Dalla Chiesa, but from men in uniform who had recently lived through the assassination of Beppe Montana, the rumor and accusation that followed Marino's death, and now the murder of Ninni and Roberto Antiochia. These uniformed policemen jostled the minister of the interior so roughly that at the end of the service he had to escape from a side exit and proceed immediately to the airport for Rome.

President Cossiga took my arm and whispered tensely, "Be my escort, Mayor. Be my escort." We walked through two walls of uniforms, the men red-eyed with grief. Like a wave, the shouting stopped and then resumed again as we passed by.

| | |

By now, Palermo was full of journalists, scavenger birds waiting for the next illustrious corpse. Every Italian newspaper had sent its best reporters, who filed one story after another on the tensions within the police and the judiciary, the rumors about the Mafia's next target, and the insecurity of the new mayor.

At one point, a German journalist was ushered into my office for an interview. "Mr. Mayor," he said. "I've just been to police headquarters and do you know what they call you there?"

"No, I don't."

"They call you 'the Walking Corpse.' They're convinced that you're next."

It was a chilling moment. It had been a long time since I took sides in this civil war. This was the first time I saw the possible consequences of my decision to play a role in the contest between the forces of law and those of chaos. I knew that if I didn't manage to build some sort of movement for change and renewal, it would be the end for me.

I began by trying to liberate the city from an age-old culture of "belonging." I am referring to the very Sicilian idea that if one belonged to a certain family, or clan, or confraternity, one could command special rights. Against this notion, it was necessary to show that the city government respected everybody's rights equally and would grant no special favors. Shortly after I had become mayor, a delegation came to my office. Its spokesman stepped forward and began: "Mr. Mayor, I'm a member of your party and I voted for you…"

I immediately rang for one of my assistants and told him, "Please show this gentleman out. I'll continue the meeting with the others."

In addition to sending out these initial signals, we tried to tackle the many everyday problems that chronically afflicted Palermo. We were, after all, a city that ostensibly had a theater, the extraordinary Teatro Massimo, but didn't really have a theater since the Massimo had been closed for "restoration" for years. We had a Municipal Public Transport Company but almost no transport, since the number of buses was minimal. We had schools but no school buildings, the students being forced to attend makeshift classes in private apartment buildings which the municipality rented at enormous cost from suspect individuals.

One of the first things I took in hand was the question of the contract for streets and sewers, not only because it was a scandal but also because the city needed proper service, the conditions of many of its streets being disastrous and of its sewers even worse. I worked to prepare a public contract for these services. The lowest bid came from a new company. We immediately signed a contract with it to provide street and sewer services at an immeasurably lower cost than the previous eternally renewed contracts.

Then, predictably, came the equal and opposite reaction, as it would whenever we managed to accomplish something. In a city where unemployment was epidemic, signing this legitimate public contract also meant that hundreds of workers of the old contractors would lose their jobs. People behind the scenes inflamed the workers' legitimate anxiety, and soon there were daily demonstrations in front of the Palazzo delle Aquile. Families with children banging drums, blowing whistles, shouting and chanting. I saw a banner with the words "The Mafia gives work." And once again, I heard that chilling cry: "Long live the Mafia!"

I called Rome and indicated that this was not a labor problem, but a Mafia problem. Within a short time, a special law was passed by Parliament allowing the company that had submitted the winning bid to hire the workers it would need directly from the old company without having to go through the bureaucratic shuffle of taking those on the official unemployment lists first. The demonstrations stopped.

| | |

I tried to do all this as loudly as possible, having learned over the previous few years that silence and isolation were dangerous. Yet while I was as public as possible in my official life, I tried to be invisible in my private life. Our family existed exclusively within the walls of the small apartment I shared with Milli and our daughters. It almost seemed as if we were alone together. There is not *one* photograph taken of my wife together with me at any public ceremony or reception in those years; Milli and the girls *never* traveled in my car with me. I had erased their existence as public people, which allowed me to retain the comforting illusion that they were less at risk. Milli recently reminded me of an incident that illustrates exactly how separate we were during that time. Typically I went to the same Mass as she did, but arrived separately and sat in a pew distant from hers. She told me that as I walked in on this particular Sunday, surrounded by my bodyguards, a young man sitting in front of her turned to the girl next to him and said in a loud whisper, "Look! Isn't that the mayor?"

The girl craned her head and had a good look, then answered: "Yes, it's the mayor." Then she asked as an afterthought, "Is he married?"

"No, he's not married," her companion replied.

Milli, sitting behind them, found herself thinking, "And who am *I* then?"

For years, nobody came to dinner or was invited to our house, and I never went to dinner or was a guest in anybody's home. Now, fortunately, things have changed, but at that time my decision, which some thought excessive and obsessive, saved me from being in places where I might have inadvertently met with the wrong person, someone who would later come back to haunt me.

| | |

In October 1985, I got a phone call from the office of the minister of the interior, telling me that the following morning a military plane would be taking me and some unnamed "other persons" to Rome for a meeting with Minister Scalfaro. When I boarded, I saw that the others were three investigating magistrates: Giovanni Falcone, Paolo Borsellino and Antonino Caponnetto. I knew who they were, but I had never met them personally before.

Antonino Caponnetto was an elderly, frail-looking, bald-headed man with gentle, large gray eyes recessed in a refined face. When Rocco Chinnici was murdered, this quiet yet tenacious magistrate had volunteered to come from a comfortable job in Florence to step into his shoes. Caponnetto had Sicilian roots—his parents had emigrated to Tuscany when he was little—and in returning to his birthplace he was exchanging a large home and a full social life for a room in military barracks without his family.

It was Caponnetto who took Chinnici's idea of an antimafia "pool" and formalized its structure.* Information would be "pooled" among a group of investigators and prosecutors whose shared insights and knowledge would not disappear or have to be laboriously reconstructed if one of them should be killed. The Antimafia Pool had started working on the "Report of the 162" drawn up by the police back in 1982, but then, with Tommaso Buscetta's confessions in 1984 and the mass arrests they triggered, followed by other confessions and more arrests, the investigation had broadened until it became a massive probe into years of Mafia criminality. Now the pool was preparing a grand trial against the Mafia which would be known as the Maxitrial because of the number of defendants: 476. Previously, Mafiosi had been tried as individuals and generally acquitted because of *omertà*, the code of silence that intimidated witnesses. But now they would be tried jointly because of the new law that recognized the Mafia as a conspiracy, and the code of silence was no longer strictly observed.

I came to respect, and later to love, Caponnetto; and like other Palermitans, I soon came to love Giovanni Falcone and Paolo Borsellino, too. Our stars were in alignment when Caponnetto brought these two men into prominence.

Falcone and Borsellino had both been born in the Kalsa, an old Arab quarter of the city. (The name derives from the Arabic *Al Khalisah*, or "elected.") They had known each other as kids and played soccer in that Piazza Magione which is the site of the beautiful Arab-Norman church where I was married. Their families were affected by the deterioration in Palermo's civic life. The

---

* The story of Falcone, the Antimafia Pool, and the pursuit of the Corleonesi has been told in absorbing detail by Alexander Stille in his fine book *Excellent Cadavers* (Random House, 1995). Stille has been one of the most perceptive observers of the fight against Cosa Nostra.

Borsellino home was eventually taken over by squatters. The place where Falcone had grown up was demolished to make way for one of those unique Palermo phenomena: a road that was never built.

The crumbling, narrow streets of the Kalsa, once the fishermen's quarter, had over the years become better known as the kingdom of Mafia boss Masino Spadaro, "King of cigarette smugglers" in the 1950s and later a great drug trafficker. Both men had become well acquainted with the enemy during their growing up. Falcone later said to me: "Luca, do you know why I'm so good at fighting the Mafia? Because I'm a Mafioso myself." What he meant, of course, was that he had grown up inside the Mafia's territory and had come to understand perfectly the Mafioso mentality. Paolo Borsellino felt something like this too, once noting that he had "breathed in the odor of the Mafia from the time I was a boy." In one of his last television interviews, given in 1992 to Swiss television, he confessed that when he was a child in Piazza Magione, he was envious of some of his schoolmates, sons of *capimafia*, because their fathers were important while his father was only a pharmacist.

They were both medium-sized men. But while Borsellino was thin and intense, a chain smoker who wore his emotions on his sleeve, Falcone had become heavy in middle age and was self-contained and even withdrawn, conveying a calm intelligence that perfectly complemented Borsellino's passion. There were other differences. Falcone had undergone a painful divorce and had become even more precise and demanding, burying himself in his work. Borsellino was married and father of three, blessed with a wicked sense of humor and impatient with constraint. (In the years to come, when he was hunted by the Mafia, he would occasionally elude his bodyguards, jump on his son's motorcycle and tear through the city.) Falcone was a Left-leaning man who had come to the issue of the Mafia through his expertise in the minute details of illegal banking transactions. Borsellino was a Right-oriented man, whose hatred of the Mafia stemmed from his determination to find the murderers of his *carabiniere* friend Emanuele Basile. But both were Sicilian to the core, stubborn and brave.

And both had the Sicilian ability to speak with their eyes. Later on, when the war with the Mafia had reached a critical point, the television show *60 Minutes* came to Palermo to film a segment. Falcone's Italian interpreter told me afterward how the American interviewer asked Falcone repeatedly if he was afraid of assassination. By this time he was sick of the question, having been asked it almost daily for years; he didn't like the idea of others vicariously participating in his possible death. So when the question came up during the interview, he looked away and gave the verbal equivalent of a shrug. The man from *60 Minutes* kept trying to get him to repeat himself more definitively while looking squarely at the camera. The interpreter, who knew that Falcone was doing this on purpose, finally said, "Don't you see that Mr. Falcone has answered the question?"

Falcone had begun his work against the Mafia in 1980 after beginning to study currency violations. When Buscetta was arrested in 1984, it was determined that Falcone was the logical one to go to Brazil to interrogate him. At first Buscetta had refused to speak to anyone, even going so far after his arrest as to take poison in an abortive effort at suicide. But Falcone won his sympathy—not by making moral appeals but simply by impressing Buscetta with his knowledge and sensibility. (One of Falcone's fellow prosecutors once said, "If Giovanni had been on the other side, he would have been a great Mafioso.") Letting Buscetta know that he was fascinated by him and his story, Falcone got him to agree to be extensively debriefed in Rome. The two men had begun an odd pas de deux in which Buscetta allowed Falcone to draw information out of him piece by piece, taking pleasure in the dynamics of the interrogation.

Much had already been learned over the years about the Mafia, a growing accretion of insights assembled by figures like Cesare Terranova and Rocco Chinnici. Buscetta was the last piece of the puzzle. He gave a complete picture of Cosa Nostra, from the initiation ceremony by which a soldier becomes a "made" man, to the hierarchy rising from the *picciotti* to the Commission. He told exactly

how the Corleonesi had risen. He also told of the Sicilians' penetration of the U.S. drug market through the "Pizza Connection,"
making sense of a comment a wiretap had caught Gaetano Badalamenti making to one of his men in New York: "They need us
because we have the import license." Buscetta's insights about the
relationship of the Mafia to the Gambinos and other American
mob families, and how they had used Midwestern pizza parlors to
set up a drug distribution network, led Falcone to a close collaboration with Rudolph Giuliani (later mayor of New York), Louis
Freeh (later FBI chief), and other federal prosecutors in America.
He agreed to let Buscetta come to the United States to be debriefed
again and live in the U.S. Witness Protection Program once the
Maxitrial was completed.

At times Falcone didn't know whether or not to believe Buscetta's
statements, which other prosecutors dismissed as disinformation.
Then Falcone asked Borsellino what he thought, knowing that his
friend had the best understanding of the Mafia mentality. When
Borsellino said that he believed Buscetta, Falcone knew the information was good.

Falcone and Borsellino. Their names were always spoken as one.
In the terrible summer of 1985, in the immediate aftermath of the
Montana-Marino-Cassarà-Antiochia tragedies, authorities picked
up a rumor in the Ucciardone jail that they were soon to be killed.
So Falcone and his fiancée, Francesca Morvillo, together with
Borsellino, his wife, son and two daughters, were quickly spirited
out of Palermo, where their safety could not be guaranteed. They
were flown to a prison on the island of Asinara off the Sardinian
coast. There they were housed in the prison guards' quarters and
there they spent their summer "holiday." The children had already
lived under armed guard. Now they faced six weeks in solitary con-
finement in a prison. Paolo's shy, introverted sixteen-year-old daughter, Lucia, started to lose her appetite and before his eyes became
seriously anorexic. He became so worried about her that when he
returned home, he began to look for ways to get out of Palermo,
away from the security constraints and the constant possibility of

death. Eventually he took a job as head of the prosecutor's office in the city of Marsala in the east of Sicily, which also had a Mafia problem, and pursued a long-distance collaboration with Falcone.

| | |

The meeting that Falcone, Borsellino, Caponnetto and I had in October 1985 with the minister of the interior in Rome cemented a relationship between Palermo and the national government in dealing with the Mafia. One law that eventually came out of these discussions established the right of family members of Mafia victims in need of sustenance to be employed in public jobs without having to go through the regular competitive exam. I gave orders that this law should immediately be applied in our city.

The meeting in Rome also forged a close bond between the Tribunal and Palazzo delle Aquile, which was slowly beginning to be seen as part of the fight against the Mafia and not as the Palace of Shame where the Mafia fed from the public trough and used the machinery of government for its own dark purposes. The four of us knew we would now be leaders in the fight ahead, they in the legal arena and I in the cultural. We agreed further that these were not really separate battles. In the metaphor I offered, there is a cart with two wheels: the wheel of justice—the law, the police, the courts, the prisons; and the wheel of civil society—an informed and responsible citizenry and a growing economy. If the wheel of justice turns without cultural and social development, the people will say (as some did during the worst days of the antimafia struggle), "We were better off when we were worse off." But if the wheel of civil society turns without justice, the risk is that an appearance of social vitality will mask the Mafia's operations. The two wheels must turn together and at the same speed if the cart is to go forward rather than in circles.

Over the next few months I became close to Borsellino, one of those rare individuals whose intensity stopped time when you were with him. Falcone was harder to know, but our relationship jelled one afternoon when he called to ask a favor. "I've decided to get married and I'd like you to celebrate my wedding," he said. "But please, I want it to be totally private without anybody knowing about it." I assured him that we Sicilians, as he knew only too well, are very good at keeping secrets, and I promised that the ceremony would be exactly as he wished. We fixed the date for a Saturday afternoon and observed the old custom of publishing the bans, but situated them in the midst of many other materials on the municipal bulletin board.

On the appointed day, when the city offices should have been closed at the end of the half-day and everybody at home for the weekend, I asked that the Register of Marriages be put on my desk, claiming that I needed to check something. The time passed and the employees waiting to lock up kept looking at the clock. Suddenly a knock on my door and a voice announced:

"Mr. Mayor… Doctor Falcone is here!"

"Yes, I was waiting for him. Show him in."

Giovanni Falcone entered with his best man, Nino Caponnetto, head of the Antimafia Pool. Shortly afterward, Francesca Morvillo, an attractive woman who was also a prosecutor, arrived with a friend. I pronounced them man and wife and my secretary recorded the marriage. Then we had a toast with a bottle of champagne that I had chilled in the refrigerator. The press didn't learn of the marriage until the newlyweds had already left for a brief honeymoon.

| | |

One of the greatest trials in Italian history was about to begin, but there was no courtroom that could possibly hold the hundreds of defendants, the dozens of lawyers and the families of victims who would testify, the judge and jury, not to mention the press and the general public. It was not just a matter of a large enough courtroom; there was also the question of security. To transport hundreds of Mafiosi every day to and from the Ucciardone prison through the center of the city would be to invite attack. So it was decided that a new courtroom, specifically designed for the Max-itrial, would be built alongside the prison—a "rib" of the Ucciar-done protected by high iron gates.

There were still a host of problems. The courtroom had to be bomb-proof. (We finally settled on huge blocks of reinforced concrete built to withstand a direct hit by an antitank missile.) It had to keep the hundreds of defendants in different barred "cages" so they would not conspire with or kill each other or be able to menace the public. The common area of the courtroom had to be large enough to hold all those who would become part of the legal process, including living quarters for the jury during its sequestration. There had to be a protected garage so that the prosecutors and judges could enter and leave the building without being targeted. There had to be strict, high-tech security including x-rays and identity checks.

Unbelievably for those accustomed to Italian bureaucracy, the Bunker Courtroom, as it soon became known, met all these challenges. It was actually a model of engineering, and the fact that it was built at enormous cost yet in a relatively short time proved that there was a new commitment on the part of the state to contend with the Mafia.

But then, in late November 1985, after prosecutors had filed the forty-two-volume indictment for the Maxitrial, the Greek tragedy stalking Sicily produced another irony. Paolo Borsellino was being driven home for lunch in his armored car, when the escort car leading the way scraped a parked car on Via Libertà, causing the driver to lose control and slam into a bus stop full of young schoolchildren laughing and chattering as they waited to go home. As Borsellino's driver swerved and screeched away, the other bodyguards leapt out of the escort cars with drawn guns. Everything had happened so quickly that for the first few terrible seconds they thought there had been an attack. They were confronted with a scene of horror. Two students, a boy named Biagio and a girl named Giuditta, had been killed instantly, a third was very seriously hurt and many had minor injuries.

It was the opportunity that the fellow travelers of the Mafia had been waiting for. Immediately they initiated a whispering campaign that eventually found expression on the local editorial pages. The prosecutors have made Palermo into an "armored city," the charge went; their security precautions are excessive and unnecessary; the sirens disturb peace-loving citizens and their cars murder children. Yes, it was bad before, when the Mafia was murdering people; but now it is worse. Our lives and the lives of our children are endangered by these antimafia personalities. Where is our "normality"? Where is that "European city" Mayor Orlando keeps promising?

I went to the site of the accident. I saw the bloody pavement, the mute horror in the eyes of the students who had survived. Back at the office, my phone rang incessantly with demands that I proclaim Palermo a "city in mourning." But I knew that if I did this, the mourning would be not so much *for* the students as *against* the prosecutors, the *carabinieri*, the police, and most of all against the changes that were beginning to germinate in civil society. I announced that I would not proclaim an official state of mourning, but because the students' deaths were like the deaths of members of my own family, I would go into *personal* mourning, and I urged every other Palermitan to do likewise.

The waiting room of Villa Sofia, the hospital where the injured young people were being treated (the same one where President Mattarella had been taken after being shot), was crowded with policemen and prosecutors, all of them with devastated looks on their faces. They had not entered the ward where the injured were being treated because they feared offending the mothers and fathers holding their children's hands. I made them go in and took them from bed to bed so they could express their sorrow and solidarity. Biagio's funeral took place in Carini, a small village near Palermo, Giuditta's in her family's parish church in the city. (Ironically, Giuditta was the daughter of a high-ranking police officer.) Paolo Borsellino stood next to me at the funeral Mass. He was broken by the deaths. When we joined hands for the Our Father, Borsellino's grief radiated from his skin like heat.

For the next few weeks, Paolo spent hours every day beside the bed of the student who was in a coma. He happened to be a personal friend of the child's family. The parents told him that they would never, not even if their son died, hold him responsible for what had happened. But Borsellino agonized over the child and prayed at the bedside, communicating his strong faith to everyone nearby. In time the boy awoke from his coma and started down the road to recovery.

While the little boy was still hospitalized, the Mafia marshaled its civic assets to get the people to take to the streets and unleash a strong attack against the rule of law and civic order trying to take hold in Palermo. I could see the dialogue taking form: were we better off now that the fight had been joined than we had been before? It seemed to me that the outcome might go either way. In the end, the people chose to defend the state, represented by the prosecutors and my administration. In their school assemblies, students proclaimed that the Mafia was responsible for the deaths of Biagio and Giuditta, and their parents agreed. This was a small but important moment in our movement for civic renewal.

As it became clear that causing a backlash would not bring victory, the Mafia returned to sending messages the old way. Early in December, just as the Maxitrial was about to get under way, they killed an old man coming out from Mass with his mother and sister. It was Leonardo Vitale, the first of the *pentiti*, whom the police had deemed insane twelve years earlier when he came forward to tell of the inner workings of the Mafia. Why was he killed now, this irrelevant old man? It was not because he had any more information to give. It was a message to Buscetta (who was now a household name in Italy as a result of the publication of the indictment), to Contorno, and to all the others who might be tempted to join them: if they stood up in court, there would be a price.

| | |

The Italian legal system has a provision allowing injured parties in a legal proceeding to be present as *parte civile*, which might be translated as "civil plaintiff." If, for instance, somebody is murdered, the family of the victim can be named as a civil plaintiff in the case against the accused murderer. Frequently the civil plaintiff's request for damages is merely symbolic, and the plaintiff's attorneys are present primarily to spur the prosecutor to work to get a conviction.

To prevent our citizens from seeing the Maxitrial as an abstract legal proceeding and to further the idea that the city of Palermo and all its inhabitants—not just those murdered on its streets—had been injured by Mafia criminality, I decided to become a civil plaintiff at the Maxitrial. My announcement was regarded as quixotic by some, and was greeted with derision by the Mafia lawyers. But the honest citizens saw it differently. Every day I heard them murmur encouragement, although not too loudly, as I walked among them: "You're right!" "We're with you!" "Get the bastards!"

A few days before the trial, the City of Palermo called a "National Assembly Against the Mafia." This was to show that we were not alone, and that the whole country had a stake in what was about to happen. Hundreds of mayors and local administrators from all over Italy came to Palazzo delle Aquile and turned its council chamber, for years a symbol of the power and intrigues of Mafiosi, into a fulcrum of the fight against them, finally waged at the national level. In my welcoming speech to Francesco Cossiga, the president of the Republic, I said simply, "Palermo is the capital of the Mafia, but Palermo intends to become the world's *anti*mafia capital." Shortly afterward, I called a press conference to announce that as civil plaintiff, the city would be represented by a legal team of three, headed by one of the greatest Roman lawyers, Giovanni Maria Flick, an expert in organized crime, who many years later would become minister of justice and then a member of the Italian Constitutional Court. He had accepted the case on one condition: that he was not to be paid, not even for the large expenses he incurred in traveling back and forth between Rome and Palermo during the next two years.

I suppose that I, like any other Catholic, have a strong belief that this world is inhabited by children of light and children of darkness. And for years I had been pessimistic, but now I had a growing conviction that the forces of light were finally mobilizing in my wounded land.

7

On the opening day of the Maxitrial, February 10, 1986, a heavy rain fell on the roadblocks scattered through the city, on the more than three thousand soldiers and the two army tanks standing outside the Bunker Courtroom, on the helicopters hovering low in the sky, and on the seemingly endless line of citizens passing through security checkpoints to enter the public gallery. They exuded an air of gaiety despite the foul weather. Today they would see the Mafiosi who had lorded it over them so long in cages. Today they would see the first cracks appear in the edifice of political dominion that the Mafia had been building in Sicily for the past hundred years.

As I entered the courtroom, I saw the area reserved for the hordes of journalists who had come to Palermo from almost every country in the world, making our streets into a Tower of Babel. Taking my place in the section designated for civil plaintiffs and their lawyers, I passed by the Mafiosi staring out from behind bars with hatred glinting in their eyes. A ripple of whispers passed from cage to cage:

U sinnacu! Talé, talé, u sinnacu! "The mayor! Look, look, the mayor!"

They had nothing else to say, but their lawyers had no hesitancy in expressing contempt on their behalf. When I stood up facing the court with my back to the cages, to confirm my presence, one of them caustically said that the mayor of Palermo should concentrate on cleaning the streets and making the buses run on time, rather than hounding poor defendants!

There was nothing unexpected in seeing me there as a civil plaintiff, or the Dalla Chiesa family, or the widow of Cesare Terranova, or the representatives of fallen *carabinieri* or the state police. But nobody expected to see a short, plump, elderly lady dressed all in black, clutching a small black handbag, with her silvering hair drawn into a tight bun at the nape of her neck, walk determinedly into the courtroom and pull a large framed photograph out of a plastic bag.

Unnè la giustizia? "Where is justice?" she demanded loudly as she looked about the room.

Vita Rugnetta was her name. She looked like a character out of a Rossellini movie about rural Sicily. Mrs. Rugnetta had the proud bearing of one of those women with a "man of honor" in her family. But her entire world had crashed when she was shown her adored only son's dead body, found in the trunk of a car parked in front of police headquarters. Antonino Rugnetta, a low-level Mafioso in training, had been a casualty of the Corleonesi. He had been subjected to the particularly brutal form of murder they had used on opponents during the Second War: the *incaprettatura* ("death of the goat"), in which the victim's arms and feet are tied in an arch behind his back with the rope passing round his neck. He was also shot, but he probably died the long, atrocious death of the *incaprettati* as his leg muscles tired and his feet lowered, slowly choking him.

This small woman who stepped into the courtroom asking about justice was dramatically breaking one of the Mafia's oldest taboos. It was possible to turn to another Mafioso for the vendetta if one had been wronged, but *never* to the state. Yet here she was, in full view of the world's press with her *J'accuse*.

Mrs. Rugnetta owned a small furniture shop in one of the narrow alleys of the historical center of Palermo. Her son had supported her, and since his death, this had been her only means of livelihood. But from the day she stepped into the Bunker Court-room and asked for justice, she did not sell a single piece of furniture. Nothing. Not even the cheapest of stools. The *capomafia* of the area had imparted strict orders: nobody was to be a customer at Vita Rugnetta's shop. Yet for years to come, long after the Maxitrial was over, she stubbornly opened her door every morning at nine o'clock. Dressed in black and surrounded by her unsold furniture, she sat the entire day in front of the shop before a small shrine of which the centerpiece was the silver-framed photograph of her son. Her debts grew but the shop remained open, thanks to those of us who saw that open shop as an important banner against the Mafia.

In stepping forth, Vita Rugnetta was only the first in what became a parade of women asking for justice. One of the Mafia's most important assets was the malicious fantasy that they upheld traditional Sicilian values, chief among them the importance of family. So when women began to criticize the Mafia, eventually founding an organization called Women Against the Mafia, a large piece of Cosa Nostra's own Berlin Wall came tumbling down.

| | |

The Maxitrial was still at the initial stages of judicial skirmishing when, ten days after its opening, someone rushed up to me and excitedly whispered that Michele Greco had been arrested! The *carabinieri*, in a secret operation involving over four hundred men, had arrested Greco at dawn in a country house in the Madonie mountains, east of Palermo.

The news swept through the city like wildfire. Now "the pope" of the Mafia would be there, in a cage with the others in the Bunker facing his judges! Michele Greco who for years had used his estate at Croceverde Giardini, a suburb on the outskirts of Palermo, to host members of many of the city's great families, politicians, ecclesiastics and even magistrates and other representatives of the forces of law and order! That Michele Greco who had also hosted Mafia dinners, held Mafia summits and enjoyed shooting parties and barbecues on his veranda while those who functioned as his soldiers were on a different part of the estate murdering other men of honor hostile to him and the Corleonesi—he would finally appear in court. And when this "pope," an innocuous-looking, elderly "country gentleman," was called to face the court and be questioned, he commenced by saying, as he spread out his open hands, *La violenza non fa parte della mia dignità.* It was a typical Mafia construction: "Violence and my dignity live separate lives."

Later we would realize that Totò Riina, the power behind his throne, had offered Greco up so the legal world would believe that now, with the "boss of bosses" in captivity, the case was solved. But even that knowledge wouldn't have restrained our work. Paolo Borsellino, a student of Mafia symbolism, became very excited in the early stages of the Maxitrial when Michele Greco's son walked into the spectator's gallery and an ordinary citizen loudly said "Hah!" as he passed by. It was a single syllable, but Paolo felt that this disrespectful "Hah" said volumes about what was happening in our city.

| | |

As the trial began, every interview, particularly those with the foreign press, ended with the same question: "Mr. Mayor, are you afraid?"

I always put the question off—not because of modesty, but because I really didn't know the answer. On account of my sickly childhood and my cosseted upbringing I had always harbored premonitions of an early death; so I was probably a bit less afraid than another man in the same position might have been. But I have an active imagination, and it wasn't difficult to think up possible scenarios involving bomb blasts, a firing squad with Kalashnikovs, even kidnapping followed by an *incaprettatura*. I received many anonymous letters filled with threats, but the serious ones—and there were many—usually didn't come to me directly. They would come to the police by means of phone calls or informers showing up in person. Or at times a bugged phone would suggest that something was in the wind.

I developed a sort of code with my bodyguards that allowed me to understand when the police considered the threats particularly grave. When the men began their shift in the morning, they were called on by their superiors to sign a specific form stating that they have been informed that Leoluca Orlando, for whose safety they are responsible, is presently considered "at particular risk." And on those days, when I got into the car they would say: "Mr. Mayor, this morning we signed." And then I'd know for sure.

But it is fair to say that whatever our bravado, we all lived in a state of wariness. My meetings with Falcone, Borsellino and Caponnetto almost always took place in the relative security of their offices. But one evening, Falcone invited me to his home. After the usual pleasantries, he turned to his wife: "Francesca, why don't you go and make Luca a coffee?"

A high-powered attorney herself who was used to being in on every secret, she hesitated for a moment.

"Come on, Francesca, we can't leave Luca without a coffee," he insisted. "Please go and make some."

As soon as Francesca had left the room, Falcone pulled a letter out from his pocket. It contained a threat addressed to him and to me. The postmark was from Germany, from Wuppertal in the Ruhr. According to the Bundes Kriminal Amt, Germany's specialists in criminality, Wuppertal is one of the three cities in their country where the Sicilian Mafia is particularly strong.

"You know," said Falcone, "this is serious."

As we heard Francesca coming back from the kitchen, Falcone quickly hid the letter and whispered, "I don't want her to be alarmed."

| | |

As the weeks went by, the Maxitrial became an endlessly drawn-out legal routine and eventually disappeared from the front page. The Bunker Courtroom operated in darkness and was surrounded by silence—precisely what the Mafia was waiting for.

Trials consist in codes, cavils, and hair splitting. Once they were out of the limelight, the defendants' lawyers began to use every trick in their trade to try to drag out the proceedings as long as possible. Their aim was to allow the period of preventive jailing possible in the Italian system to elapse so their clients would have to be released on parole (at which point, of course, most of them would immediately vanish). It was like watching an invisible duel. First the defendants began having "fits"—one sewed his lips shut (literally, with needle and thread, there in the cage!); another swallowed nails. The court ordered them to be carried out and the proceedings continued. Then it was the Mafia lawyers' turn. First they asked that *all* the hundreds of thousands of pages of evidence—over eight hundred thousand of them—be read aloud in court (which one newspaper calculated would take several years). The court agreed that the defendants had the right to make this request, but ruled that the days on which it sat for this procedure would not be subtracted from the days allowed by law for the defendants to be preventively jailed, whereupon the lawyers quickly withdrew.

During all these maneuverings, Cosa Nostra was marking time—no killings, only a few armed robberies. There was an almost unearthly hush as they lay low and waited, in obedience to the old Sicilian proverb advising citizens of a perpetually conquered land to bide their time. *Calati juncu ca passa la china.* "Bend over reed and let the flood pass you by."

And indeed—despite the fact that Tommaso Buscetta, contrary to the lawyers' expectations, flew in from the United States where he was living under the Witness Protection Program to confirm in person all he had said to Giovanni Falcone, and despite Salvatore Contorno's testimony and that of all the other informants who described, as if they were reading a shopping list, the wholesale killing and torture and the bodies melted in drums of acid so there would be no trace of *lupara bianca* victims—the attention of the media and the people wandered.

| | |

In late January 1987, Italy's oldest and most prestigious newspaper, *Il Corriere della Sera*, published an article by Leonardo Sciascia, one of the greatest Italian writers of the twentieth century. Sciascia was a Sicilian from a small town called Racalmuto in the province of Agrigento, but he had lived for several years in Paris. His novels, perhaps the most famous of which is *The Day of the Owl*, had schooled a generation of Italians in the mentality and semiotics of the Mafia. Sciascia knew little of the urban Mafia that had developed in recent years, but he understood the mentality of the rural Mafia very well. One of his best characters, the godfather of a small village, famously divides all men into four categories: *Uomini, mezzi uomini, uominicchi e quaquaraqua.* "Men, half-men, piddling little men and quacking ducks." In five words—particularly the last one, a way of indicating the brain-dead followers of Cosa Nostra— he had achieved a masterly portrayal of the Mafia boss's worldview.

Sciascia's article mentioned Paolo Borsellino by name, pointing out that he had been chosen for his job as head of the prosecutor's office in Marsala, a frontline town in the fight against the Mafia, over another prosecutor with greater seniority. (No mention was made of the fact that this more senior prosecutor had no experience with the Mafia.) Sciascia also referred to an unnamed mayor who deliberately put himself in the limelight by giving interviews and speaking in schools and conferences against the Mafia, knowing that by doing so he was furthering his career and that nobody would dare to attack him for fear of being accused of being a Mafioso. These men and others like them, said Sciascia—unequivocally pointing his pen at Borsellino and myself—were "antimafia professionals" feathering their own nests through politics.

On the day after the article appeared, Milli and I were on a plane with Giovanni Falcone and his wife, Francesca, headed for Moscow where he was to meet with Soviet magistrates and detectives working in that country against organized crime, and I with municipal authorities in the capital and in Leningrad who were facing the same problem. Falcone and I commented on Sciascia's article. I told him that Sciascia's words would possibly work as the rain of the Sicilian proverb: *Quannu chiovi nescinu i cuorna ri babbaluci.* "When it rains, all the snails come out of their shells."

"Oh, yes," Falcone said. "Just you wait and see how many snails will suddenly appear now, trailing their slime."

Never had Sciascia, who ironically was a well-known opponent of the Mafia, had so many admirers. *Sciasciani* grew up like mushrooms everywhere. People who had never read a single book by Sciascia in all their lives and who in fact had never even heard of him now praised him as being so insightful. Those who would never have been able to perceive the sharpness and nuance of his beautiful prose now suddenly became literary critics singing his praises.

The furor stirred up by Sciascia's article raged on for weeks, magnified by all the newspapers. The net effect was that those of us in the growing antimafia movement were made to seem the Siamese twins of the Mafia itself. I was never clear on what Sciascia hoped to achieve by his outburst, but I have trouble believing that he meant to promote such a moral equivalence.

This was the climate in the city as we approached the national elections, to be held in late spring of 1987. As the election campaign hit full stride, one could feel the presence of the Mafia, bent on intimidating candidates. And for the first time, certain candidates of the Christian Democratic Party were targeted—that party which had, with few exceptions, represented a sure thing for the people of Our Thing. I received a report from a longtime colleague who told me that he was not being allowed to campaign in his own district; from a CD trade unionist whose car was burnt; from another whose tires had been slashed. It was very obvious that Cosa Nostra, for the first time, intended to punish that party which, after the strong stand taken by National Secretary De Mita and after my election and activities as mayor, had become to their eyes untrustworthy. In fact, the Mafia had just started turning its attention and opening its spigot of votes onto another party and its candidates.

I decided to protest against these trends by holding a rally in Corleone. The Christian Democrats had never held a rally in that town, worldwide symbol of the Mafia, because there had never been any need. The Mafia knew whom to vote for and enforced its will on the town's inhabitants.

My armored car pulled up in the large central square, and as first my bodyguards and then I got out, a small group of faithful Christian Democrat friends surrounded me. We began walking up the town's main road toward the small square in front of the town hall, once Palazzo Cammarata (named for my mother's family), where I had asked that the podium be erected. My political friends' nervousness and fear were tangible. One of them edged up closer to me and said softly:

"Luca, there's no need for you to mention the Mafia."

"Sure," I answered. "I've come to Corleone to speak of robotics!"

When I climbed up on the podium, I was alone except for my bodyguards. Nobody from the local Christian Democratic Party introduced me as the speaker. Nobody stood next to me. In front of the podium, on the small square, a handful of brave people stood their ground. All the citizens of Corleone who had come to hear me speak—and there were many—stood down on the road so that if challenged, they could answer that they had been "passing by chance" and had stopped for a moment to hear what I was saying.

"Tell those cowards who kill and then hide, that they aren't only criminals," I began. "Tell them that they aren't even Sicilians! Tell them that they are *unworthy* of being called Sicilians! If a Sicilian kills, he doesn't hide in the shadows!"

As soon as I had finished speaking, my erstwhile friends, forgetting their previous pressing invitation to stay for dinner in a country trattoria famed for its pasta and special pastries, bundled me hastily back to my car and insisted that I return to Palermo immediately for my own good.

That return journey is a sweet memory, with the beautiful Sicilian countryside bathed in the last rays of the setting sun. I had probably engaged in what the French call an *acte gratuite*, but I was bathed in a sense of fulfillment for having honored the memory of my family and ransomed my distant forefathers who unknowingly let a world come into being where the Mafia reigned supreme.

| | |

In the 1990s, the next generation of Mafia informers after Buscetta and Contorno, the most important of whom was Francesco Marino Mannoia, confirmed that in the 1987 elections Totò Riina decided to punish the Christian Democrats because they had become "unreliable" in allowing the Maxitrial to proceed. As the vote was counted, the Socialist and Radical parties had a huge increase in votes, particularly in high-density Mafia districts like Brancaccio (and at the Ucciardone prison!). It was a huge object lesson.

Although the national election theoretically had no influence on local politics, the Socialist Party denounced me, in the phrase that Sciascia had made possible, as an "antimafia professional and demagogue." As I thought of stepping down, I asked myself why the local coalition running a city must necessarily reflect the coalition running the country. Had we not been saying that the fight against the Mafia was more important than party? I decided to put out feelers to those in other parties who had seen the importance of this fight and discovered that I still could have a majority— although a thin one—excluding the Socialists but including the Greens and two leftist independents.

Almost exactly two years after I first sat in the mayor's chair, I was reelected by the new coalition, which immediately became known as the "anomalous government." Those Christian Democrat councilors who looked to Salvo Lima and his national mentor, the powerful Giulio Andreotti, as their point of reference hated me, but not wishing the party to lose its power, they agreed to obey the orders of De Mita and vote for me. Those who joined in this coalition did not know it at the time, but the "Palermo Spring," as it came to be called, had been born. The phrase came from the fact that over the next two and a half years, many came to see what was happening in our city as a parallel to what had begun to germinate in Prague under Dubcek twenty years earlier.

We began tenuous experiments in the sort of civic consciousness that was the norm in most European and American cities. The fight we were beginning to wage against the Mafia did not involve two massed armies, but rather house-to-house fighting in which we tried to recapture our civic lives neighborhood by neighborhood.

One special objective in this campaign was our schools. The situation was unimaginable in any other European city. A vast number of Palermo's schools were housed, as I have already mentioned, not in school buildings but in private apartments, which meant discomfort for the children and their teachers and huge expense for the municipality, which rented the apartments at extortionate rates, usually from Mafia owners or their fronts.

I met with headmasters and parents who complained that their children were going to school in morning and afternoon shifts in the few real school buildings we had. At the end of each of these meetings, someone would invariably inform me that there was a building next door or down the road or around the corner that was renting apartments and that this could be a solution to the double shift problem. I always heard them out and always answered that the administration would build new schools, but this would take years and much money, and in the meantime, as far as I was concerned, students would go to school not only in two shifts, but in three or even four if necessary, and we would *not* rent any more apartments. When it became clear that I did not intend to retreat from this principle, a headmaster would suddenly remember: "Well, actually… there are several classrooms at our school which have been closed for years because they need some work done. Perhaps we could open them… "

One such case was simply amazing. I had received a delegation of teachers and parents from a place called the Cep, a particularly degraded district on the periphery of the city developed during the years of the Sack of Palermo and since then abandoned to drugs and criminality. The children there all attended classes in shifts in the only existing school. The delegation had come to request that the municipality rent a building in a nearby district and then bus the children back and forth. I got someone to check on the ownership of this building and discovered that it was owned by a company with Mafia ties. A few hours later, after the delegation had left in anger when I refused its request, I was anonymously informed that in that same district there was a modern municipal school which *had never been used* and had been sitting there, closed, for years. I immediately sent someone to check and discovered that this was true. There was a school, vandalized during the years of its vacancy, but a large, functional and potentially modern school nonetheless. Some months later, after we had completed the necessary repairs, the school opened—a place owned by the people and not some shadowy individual with no interest in education—and the double shifts ended.

In Croceverde Giardini, Michele Greco's district, the municipality had for years been renting four small rooms as an elementary school, almost in front of "the pope's" own villa. The place was owned by the Prestifilippo family, one of whose members, Mario Prestifilippo, was one of the Corleonesi's most effective soldiers, having committed more than forty murders before he himself was killed. When I heard of this involvement, I immediately cancelled the contract for the apartment and ordered that the children of the area be bused to school in a nearby district, Ciaculli. Immediately afterward began the whispering campaign: "When there was the Mafia, we at least had a school… "

But then a group of citizens from Croceverde Giardini, led by their parish priest, came to me and said: "Mr. Mayor, we know that in our area it's almost impossible to rent anything which is unoccupied and not Mafia-owned…. Why then don't we try to build a school?" Researching the matter, I discovered that a particular piece of land had long since been chosen as the site of a school building, but had never been expropriated. The reason was very soon clear to me: it belonged to Mrs. Greco, the wife of "Pope" Michele. When I discovered this, I ordered that the municipal authority was to proceed with the expropriation as soon as possible.

The city government took possession of the land and we started planning the school. It was one of the most difficult ventures of those years as mayor. One day a necessary signature was missing, another day a particular stamp on some document disappeared, then someone hadn't made the calculations for the amount of cement necessary, and so on. But finally the school was finished and inaugurated. No one had to say the obvious: when the Mafia reigned in Croceverde Giardini, the children went to school in four small, dingy rooms; now that the antimafia had taken over, the children went to a modern school right in the center of their district.

The children were our future. But we were concerned about our past, too. The center of Palermo, which was also the center of our heritage, had become filthy and polluted, its streets jammed with cars that were dumped rather than parked. There was no garbage collection, the Mafia having long given this no-show job to its clients, and so Palermitans got even by throwing their trash on the streets and keeping their homes spotless. We sent in the trash collectors. We also reorganized the traffic police, which at that point resembled one of those Third World volunteer forces, without uniforms and as inefficient as it was venal. We decided to close one of the central streets, Via Principe di Belmonte, and turn it into a pedestrian mall with open air cafés, flowers, trees and shrubs. Soon the citizens of Palermo began to emerge from their fortress homes and congregate there.

Members of city government had to function not only as politicians and administrators, but as teachers too in this struggle to educate the Palermitans about their precious heritage. One person who filled this function was Letizia Battaglia, a world-famous photographer who was elected to the council as a Green and became my "Commissioner for Gardens and Quality of Life." Winner of the prestigious W. Eugene Smith Award for her photographs of the Mafia's impact on Sicily, Letizia had reported the events of our city for years, walking fearlessly through dangerous areas with her 35mm camera slung round her neck, arriving at the site of murders and massacres sometimes even before the authorities and capturing the essence of the horror, the bereavement, the solitude. Her photos were worth thousands of words describing the decay of the narrow alleys in Palermo's historical center, the poverty along with the irrepressible vitality evident in our children, the empty magnificence of the aristocracy hiding in the few remaining palazzos.

Letizia was a short, plump lady in her early fifties, with shoulder-length auburn hair, long bangs that she kept trying to push out of her eyes, and a wide, generous mouth. She knew nothing about city administration and didn't care for official procedures. But every morning at six o'clock, not always remembering to protect her hands with gloves, she was on the streets working with municipal employees as they weeded or redesigned flower beds. If a magazine wanted to hire Letizia for a shoot, its art director had to search for her in our city's abandoned gardens and parks. Or when the good weather approached, on the littered beaches, once among the best in the Mediterranean but now used as dumps for every piece of unwanted household rubbish, and dangerous to walk on because of discarded syringes.

Some dismissed her as quixotic, but Letizia believed that common access to beautiful civic spaces—the only places where everyone was equal despite their wealth—was the first step toward building a culture of respect and an appreciation of the city. She believed that if a citizen is offered a well-cared-for park or a pristine beach, he will have a stake in keeping it like that. At times, when this response was slow in coming, she became disheartened and I would find her crying quietly in some corner of a park. Yet the next morning she would be back out there again, tools in hand, full of new ideas and ready for a new battle.

Soon, visiting journalists, who had followed the consequences of the Sack of Palermo were saying to me: "You know, Mr. Mayor, I'd never noticed how beautiful Villa Bonanno is. Those magnificent palm trees!" Or: "Do you know, Mr. Mayor, that I'd never noticed there was a garden along Via Libertà. Was it always there?"

Palermo is full of the vestiges of many civilizations, many histories, all of which had been buried in corruption and destruction during the Mafia's Hundred Years' War against Sicily. We began to excavate this past.

The municipality began by buying a superb villa belonging to two Sicilian Americans, the daughters of the Prince of Niscemi, both of whom lived in New York. They needed to sell this beautiful family villa in a park-like setting, with its frescoed rooms and all its antique furniture, pictures and vases. At a time when Palermo was crushed by so many problems, many said it was folly to spend public money on a villa. Yet the Niscemi daughters had offered it at a low price, and the villa, which would have been demolished by another purchaser, was part of our heritage. So we bought it and made it the seat of city government, open to the public. Families that would never have been able to set foot in one of Palermo's aristocratic homes now come to visit it with their children, wandering through the resplendent rooms in almost hushed awe.

After the construction of shoddy high-rises on the outskirts of the city, the second phase of the Mafia-designed Town Plan that led to the Sack of Palermo foresaw the demolition of the urban center altogether. One of the documents I discovered in the municipal files is quite blunt: "It is necessary to eliminate the abomination of these buildings of the past." This included churches and palazzos from the sixteenth and seventeenth centuries, and the Arab quarters with their narrow alleys and courtyards. And once the area had been evacuated and property bought up for a song, the Mafia's speculative construction would have stepped in. It is not surprising that among the many things Tommaso Buscetta told Falcone was that when he was in Brazil in 1980, Pippo Calò, Cosa Nostra's "cashier," at the time living comfortably in Rome, urged him to return to Palermo because "very big money" would be made with the reconstruction of the historical center.

My commissioner for urban development, Renato Palazzo, and I agreed on a strategy for keeping this precious asset out of Mafia hands. At three o'clock one morning, after an endless city government meeting, Palazzo put forward his proposal to hire three prestigious architects—none of them Sicilian, to prevent conflict of interest—to draw up a new plan for the historical center that eliminated the possibility of demolition. I played the part we had agreed upon beforehand and reprimanded him angrily for coming forward with such an important proposal only "at the end of a long meeting," but then, after "cooling down," gave the proposal my full support.

The bill was approved and, picking our way through a minefield of opposition, we began to rehabilitate a public building here, a private home there. It was a drop in the ocean of decay, but a beginning. Slowly we began to restore areas like Piazza Tavola Tonda, a site near the waterfront where many buildings, over fifty years after World War II, were still pockmarked from Allied shelling.

| | |

One day I was walking through the Ballarò market, which sprawls through the narrow streets of one of the old Arab quarters with its sudden, colorful vistas of baroque glazed-tile cupolas, when I heard a voice cry out, *Curnùtu cu parra male ddu sinnacu!* "Cuckold he who speaks ill of the mayor!" It was a colorful if crude way of expressing enthusiasm, picked up in a chant by the vendors, making the entire market ring with loud, laughing voices. And sometimes, seeing the tense looks of my bodyguards, someone would confront them in strong Sicilian dialect: *'Cca u sinnacu unn' avi bisogno di scorta. Prima annu ammazzari a nuatri.* "Here the mayor doesn't need an escort. They [the Mafiosi] would have to kill us first!"

This is one of the mental snapshots I carry with me to remember the Palermo Spring. Another time, near Christmas, I went to the Vucciria, perhaps the most famous of Palermo's markets. A group of schoolchildren were crossing the Vucciria square amidst the stalls and as soon as they saw me, ignoring the threatening looks of my escort, they surrounded me, pushing between my guards, one tugging my jacket to draw my attention.

"Mayor, Mayor!" One yelled. "Remember me? You came to my school!"

Others were digging in their satchels to pull out exercise books which they proceeded to thrust under my nose:

"Mayor, my name's Salvatore... write me something!"

"I'm Rosalia, Mayor... an autograph!"

A third episode is one that I particularly cherish because in it I see a promise for the future. I found myself facing a smartly dressed, no-nonsense sort of businesswoman at an official function. She initiated a conversation that was superficial and slightly bored. My answers were almost as detached, since I recognized the tone and attitude and knew that my replies would probably be used as a pretext for ridicule and sarcasm at some future dinner party. And her next words seemed to confirm this impression.

"I frequently have Palermo entrepreneurs to dinner and sooner or later the conversation falls on you and your government."

There was a pause as she looked at me almost speculatively. "They don't like you," she continued frankly. "They say you're a xenophile, that you're proud and... that you won't accept kickbacks! Who do you think you are anyway? they ask."

Then she added: "But every time someone speaks against you, the youngest of my sons, Gabriele, strenuously takes up your defense."

"Really?" I asked. "How old is he?"

"Eleven. You went to his school and spoke to the children."

Then she looked at me thoughtfully before finishing: "You know what? You can't be my mayor… it's too late for that. But you are already my son's mayor and maybe that's good."

8

T he Bunker Courtroom was packed once again on the evening of December 16, 1987. After almost a year of litigation and more than a month of sequestration, the jury of the Maxitrial had signaled that it was ready to emerge from its chambers. Judge Alfonso Giordano would read the verdict. Spectators noted that his face and that of his co-judge, Piero Grasso, both of which had been clean-shaven at the beginning of deliberations, were now bearded.

"In the name of the Italian people..." As Giordano began, a hushed silence came over the room and never broke for the several hours he continued in his high-pitched voice. Some lower-level soldiers got off. Ignazio Salvo, whose cousin Nino had died in hiding in Switzerland, was condemned to six years. But Giordano also said the words "life sentence" in connection with the names of the nineteen most important Mafia bosses. For those who were in custody, like Michele Greco, prison doors would not open again. For others who were still on the loose, like Totò Riina and Bernardo Provenzano, the life sentence awaited their capture. In all, 2,665 years of prison were imposed and a total of 11.5 billion lire in fines was assessed.*

---

* Civil plaintiffs, including the city, were entitled to a refund of their judicial expenses, and were recognized as eligible for damage compensation.

The state had spoken. Almost immediately, Cosa Nostra, which for almost two years had been lying low and waiting to see what would happen, passed its own verdicts. The very same night on which he had been acquitted, for instance, thirty-five-year-old Antonino Ciulla, a minor Mafioso, was killed on his doorstep, clutching a bottle of champagne he had bought to celebrate with his family. Eventually, Cosa Nostra "corrected" seventeen other Maxitrial acquittals it didn't agree with.

The Mafia was back to business as usual, and that business, of course, was murder. The next illustrious corpse was that of Giuseppe Insalaco, assassinated in his car late one night about a month after the sentences were handed out—"Peppuccio" who had been mayor for four hectic months and since then had been predicting that sooner or later "they" would get him.

I was in my office when I heard the news of Insalaco's assassination. I felt that I had reached the end of a road I had walked since I began working with Piersanti Mattarella ten years earlier. There was an undoubted foolishness about "Peppuccio," yet his murder embodied a truth it had taken so long for all of us in the antimafia to understand. The link between the Mafia and politics, which before had seemed a one-way street, actually went both ways. The Mafia used politics to carry out its business, and politics used the Mafia to reinforce its power. By the time he was killed, Giuseppe Insalaco was totally powerless and represented no danger to Cosa Nostra, but he did threaten the political structure of which he had been a part. At the time of his murder he had been working on a manuscript, he had announced with characteristic braggadocio, about "the good and the bad" in Palermo's political world. It is easy to see how certain politicians might have worried that Insalaco could become their equivalent of Tommaso Buscetta. We knew that the Mafia used its political connections to get what it wanted; were the politicians now using the Mafia to do their killing?

When I went to the mortuary, I found that I was the only politician there. Insalaco's family was there, but not one of the many party colleagues who had hung onto his sleeve during the several years he was commissioner and mayor showed up. Poor Peppuccio, a fixture in some of the ambiguous political salons of the city when he was alive, had no friends in death.

On the day of Insalaco's funeral, Natale Mondo, the policeman who had escaped with his life in the hailstorm of bullets that killed Ninni Cassarà and Roberto Antiochia, was murdered as he was about to open his wife's toy shop. Because he had survived Ninni's death, Mondo had automatically been accused of being the mole within the police, and was thus forced, in defending himself, to speak of the investigative work he had been doing. On Cassarà's orders, he had infiltrated the Mafia family of his area, on the track of heroin traffickers. That this was true had been proven by entries in Ninni's own diary. So while Palermo's citizens eventually forgave Mondo for being alive, Cosa Nostra did not. They waited for the Maxitrial to be over and then they rubbed him out.

| | |

In the spring of 1988, Antonino Caponnetto, now regarded with great respect as the godfather of the Antimafia Pool, still had two years to go before retirement. But his time in Palermo—years of isolation passed in the security barracks where he and the others were forced to live—had worn down an already frail physique. Giovanni Falcone encouraged him to return to his home and family in Florence. From Marsala, where he headed the prosecutor's office, Paolo Borsellino added his grateful voice: "Go, Nino. There's a limit to the sacrifices we can ask of you." His health was such that he was finally forced to send his resignation to the governing body of the judiciary, the Superior Council of Magistrates.

Caponnetto's only doubts centered on the question of his successor. Giovanni Falcone was the obvious choice to replace him. But would he, in the byzantine politics that ruled Italy's political world, get the job? Caponnetto had recommended Falcone, and Falcone had applied for the post. We all thought that the Superior Council would vote in his favor. But charges of "protagonism" began to be heard: like me and certain others, it was whispered, Falcone was making a profession out of his antimafia philosophy. He was using it as a ladder to personal power. Although this disinformation was obviously spread by the Mafia itself, it was repeated so often that it began to gain traction in the press and in public opinion. By one vote, the seventeen-member council chose another candidate, a man named Antonino Meli, over Falcone. Caponnetto was unable to do anything to affect the process. Like the rest of us, he watched impotently as his natural heir was passed over in favor of a man who not only was too old at sixty-eight, but was regarded as irascible and egotistical, and lacking any particular understanding of the Mafia.

Meli proved that the rumors about him were right when, shortly after taking office, he set about dismantling the Antimafia Pool. He decreed that the magistrates would no longer have special areas of responsibility; they would all handle the cases that came in. No special expertise in the Mafia was acknowledged any longer. Falcone, now recognized internationally as the expert on the Mafia, could just as easily find himself prosecuting a purse-snatcher as a *capomafia*.

So instead of swiftly building on the dramatic success of the Maxitrial, the Investigating Magistrates' Office became a center of infighting, with Meli's faction claiming that the Mafia had been tamed and pushing for "normalization," while those around Falcone insisted that now was the moment to drive a stake through Cosa Nostra's heart. As dissension took over, ongoing investigations into the Mafia languished or dead-ended. The extraordinary achievements of the previous years and the encyclopedic knowledge of the Mafia phenomenon which they had generated seemed never to have happened. As one member of the Antimafia Pool had put it: "Before, we looked at single little pieces of stone that meant nothing; then, when we put them all together, they fell into place and became a revealing mosaic." Now, however, they were back to looking at isolated little pieces of stone.

About this time, I agreed to accompany a priest from a high-density Mafia area in Palermo who was taking a group of schoolchildren to Rome to attend a papal audience and then be received by the president of the Italian Republic. When we went to the Quirinal Palace, seat of the president, I arranged to speak privately with President Cossiga. I poured out my doubts and frustrations about what was happening in Palermo—not only the chaos at the Tribunal but especially the implications of Insalaco's assassination. Cossiga listened noncommittally, and then escorted me to his door.

"I recently reread your paper on administrative coordination," he said as I was leaving, referring to something I had written years earlier while teaching law. "Why don't you return to writing books on law?"

Was he suggesting that I was exaggerating the Mafia threat, or giving me a warning? It was hard to know.

| | |

It was mid-July and I was in the cloister of the Church of San Nicola in Agrigento with Paolo Borsellino and Alfredo Galasso, the lawyer who had represented the Dalla Chiesa family at the Maxitrial. We had been invited to celebrate the publication of a book on judicial investigations into the Mafia of Agrigento. It was an important occasion because it meant expanding attention on the Mafia beyond the boundaries of Palermo.

Intense and angry over developments in the Palermo Investigating Magistrates' Office, Borsellino spoke extemporaneously—and quite bluntly—for almost an hour: "We are in a climate of general demobilization.... They are dismantling the Antimafia Pool of Palermo.... " It was an electrifying moment for the audience, but only two journalists were present, one from *La Repubblica* and the other from the Communist paper *L'Unità*. This second reporter went to interview Borsellino the following day in Marsala, where Paolo spelled out his feelings even more explicitly: "Until a short time ago all the antimafia investigations, precisely because of the unity of Cosa Nostra, were strongly centralized in the pool....

Today, instead, the cases are dispersed in a thousand rivulets....The police, since the killings of policemen Cassarà and Montana, have remained decapitated. The investigative staff is zeroed."

This time his words didn't go unnoticed. The new group in charge of the Investigating Magistrates' Office accused him of being in a conspiracy with his friend Falcone to attack Falcone's boss, Antonino Meli. The press reported the resulting charges and countercharges, and finally the argument became loud enough that it was heard in Rome. President Cossiga asked the Superior Council of Magistrates (CSM) to investigate Borsellino's charges that the fight against the Mafia was being suspended.

The CSM began interrogating all the magistrates concerned, continuing nonstop through the whole day and night. In a four-page letter, Falcone broke the silence he had maintained since being passed over to head the pool, and after bitterly condemning the shelving of the Mafia investigations, he asked to be reassigned to another office. The CSM, on a split vote, rejected his request and denied Borsellino's claims.

On the following day, I got a call: "Luca, have you heard what they did?" It was Falcone. "I'm worried. Help us Luca, help us because I'm afraid for our safety."

I was stunned. Falcone was the quintessential man of understatement. Never before had I heard him say anything like this, and I didn't know how to respond.

"Giovanni, call the president," I stammered. "Call Cossiga. With your international prestige he has to listen to you!"

I knew what he was saying. In rejecting Borsellino's charges and implying that the Mafia had been contained, the official world was in effect cutting him and Paolo adrift. If past experience proved anything, it was that such isolation was a prelude to murder.

I knew that something had to be done if we were to avoid another summer of blood. A few minutes after putting down the phone with Falcone, I called a press conference, which despite the short notice was crammed with journalists. I was tenser than I had ever been before. I said that if they told the people what the invisible political world was doing to Falcone and all the others who had fought the Mafia, "we might manage to avoid another state funeral." The state was not committed to fighting the Mafia, I said, because aspects of the state *protected* the Mafia. I had never been so explicit.

The following morning I was in Sferracavallo, at my family's seaside villa, when I received another phone call from Falcone.

"Luca, have you seen the papers?"

I hadn't yet.

"You haven't?" continued Falcone. "They're all carrying your statement. You've focused attention. And maybe this will help save my life and Paolo's life. Thank you."

| | |

A few days after my press conference, I was called by the Ministry of the Interior and told that it had information suggesting that my family and I were at particularly high risk at that moment. I was strongly advised to take a long holiday—preferably abroad. Within days Milli and I and our daughters Eleonora and Leila went to Tbilisi in Georgia, at that time still part of the Soviet Union.

Admittedly this was an odd destination, although the Communist world was one of the few asylums not penetrated by the Mafia. I decided to go there because of an incident that had occurred a few months earlier. I had been rummaging through some archival materials in the city offices and had discovered that the first written grammar of the Georgian language had been assembled in 1600 by a Palermitan monk, Father Francesco Maria Maggio, who had done missionary work in that country. Fascinated, I began digging up more and more information, including Father Maggio's journal of his travels. I contacted the mayor of Tbilisi and told him about these discoveries, with the result that Palermo and Tbilisi became "sister cities." This was the first time that Palermo had done this—it is easy to see why there hadn't been many requests from other cities seeking this honor—so when I had to choose a place to go while things calmed down at home, I thought that we might as well go someplace where we had at least a distant connection.

During the month we were in Georgia, the authorities saw to it that we were not merely protected, but had a real holiday. Suspended in generous isolation, we were treated with an affectionate hospitality that surprised me. Every time I asked my Georgian hosts for news of Italy and Sicily, they would answer that I needed to eat, drink, sleep and not worry about anything so remote. Finally, for the first time in many years, I let go of my worries about home. We stayed in a series of enormous and very secure state houses, and each time we arrived at a new one, Eleonora and Leila would eagerly explore them and then exclaim: "Oh Daddy, this house is at least ten times the size of ours!"

We toured Georgia, a beautiful land, in interminably long motor-cades that sounded their horns and at times even used loudspeakers to warn cars and pedestrians to clear the road so we could move faster and in security. Sometimes we flew in official Ilyushins if the distances were great. My visits throughout Georgia and then to Moscow gave me an opportunity to see glasnost before it was buried in the rubble of the Berlin Wall a year later.

Also a cocktail of different races and cultures, Georgia was in many ways similar to Sicily. The Georgians had submitted to the tsars' military pressure, but considered the Russians barbarians. I was amazed and delighted to find that one of the Georgian children's favorite fairytales had been used by Luigi Pirandello as the basis for one of his most famous short stories, "La Giara." The greatest Sicilian writer of the twentieth century, winner of the Nobel Prize, had taken the idea from Georgian tradition and nobody was any the wiser!

| | |

Hearing that the danger of assassination had diminished, we returned home to find that instead of focusing on the unsolved murders of all our illustrious corpses, the new head of the Investigating Magistrates' Office, acting on a Socialist lawyer's brief, had decided to open an investigation into my statements at the August press conference. I was officially called in for questioning. I had said there were connections between the political world and the world of the Mafia. Who were these connections? They wanted names.

"The collusion between politicians and Mafia," I answered during the interminable interrogation, "is written in the thousands of pages of the Parliamentary Antimafia Commission's reports and their minutes. They are public documents and everybody, including yourselves, can read them." Then I handed those questioning me several heavy volumes comprising the final reports of two consecutive Parliamentary Antimafia Commissions. Politicians, journalists, heads of the army and security, entrepreneurs, publishers: there were plenty of names in those volumes and more than sufficient material to direct an investigation.

"Orlando, demagogue, as usual!" thundered the Socialist press. "He talks, talks, talks, but names no names."

The uphill climb of my administration at times became too steep. With each passing day it was more difficult to get a deliberation approved in the city council, our opponents doing their utmost to stall any project so as to be able to turn around and smugly say that we talked a lot but did nothing. The Socialists were always spoiling for a fight, but all too frequently this opposition came from within the ranks of my own party—from the Andreotti faction, which had voted for my coalition for party reasons but was clearly obeying orders to make our life as difficult as possible until the time was right to trip us up.

The atmosphere became surreal when Salvatore Contorno, the informer who had begun speaking to authorities soon after Tommaso Buscetta and whose revelations had caused a second massive wave of Mafia arrests, was discovered to be in Palermo instead of in the U.S. Witness Protection Program. The police had been on the tracks of Gaetano Grado, a cousin of Contorno's and like him part of the losing faction of Cosa Nostra. Grado was suspected of being behind a series of revenge killings of members of the winning Corleonesi clan. When the police raided Grado's house, they found themselves face to face with Contorno. It turned out that the Criminal Police had known of Contorno's decision to leave the United States, but because his only obligation was a twice-weekly telephone call, they were not aware of his presence in Sicily and in Palermo—the one place in the world where he should never again have set foot if he valued life.

Soon, anonymous letters began turning up in government and newspaper offices. They openly accused Giovanni Falcone along with his colleague Gianni De Gennaro—who had worked closely with Falcone, Borsellino, Rudolph Giuliani and the FBI, and would be appointed chief of the Italian Police a few years later—of bringing Contorno back as a "state killer" against the Corleonesi. They also threw mud on Giuseppe Ayala, the former public prosecutor in the Maxitrial and close friend and colleague of Falcone. The letters of "the Crow" (the anonymous author was named after a character in a film by French director Clouzot, in which the elderly protagonist spent his time writing anonymous letters) were discovered to have been typed on a typewriter in the Investigating Magistrates' Office. Once again there seemed to be an effort on the part of the official world to destroy the credibility of some of the most significant figures in the battle against Cosa Nostra.

In this poisoned climate, Carla Del Ponte, at the time a Swiss prosecutor and today president of the International Court for Crimes Against Humanity in The Hague, came to Palermo in June 1989. Del Ponte had been working with Falcone on complex investigations into the laundering of Mafia money through Swiss banks. She joined Falcone at his office. The plan was that they would work on issues involving the international spread of the Mafia in the morning and then after lunch go for a swim at the summer house he had rented on the rocky coast near Mondello. But providentially the morning dragged too long, delaying their walk to the seacoast. Just before they were supposed to pass by, one of Falcone's guards saw a scuba diver's bag on the rocks. When he opened it, he found that it contained a remote-control triggering device and fifty-eight sticks of plastic explosive, enough to blow a huge crater in the beach.

As soon as the news reached me, I called an assembly in which I condemned this cowardly attempt on Falcone's life. As I finished, a friend sitting next to me said, "Luca, you never used the word *Mafia*."

"Of course," I immediately answered. "This is mainly politics. Politicians using the Mafia."

Three weeks later, in an interview with a correspondent for the newspaper *L'Unità*, Falcone confirmed my thoughts: "We are faced with extremely refined minds which are attempting to guide certain actions of the Mafia. There are perhaps connections between the heads of Cosa Nostra and concealed centers of power which have other interests.... I am watching the repeat performance of what produced the death of General Dalla Chiesa.... The script is the same. One only has to have eyes to see it."

9

One morning early in 1990, Falcone called and asked me to come by his office. When I arrived, he took me to a table where a very odd map of Palermo was rolled out. The map had been drawn using information from a ledger found in the hideout of a member of the Madonia family, one of the leading families in the Corleonesi faction. This document contained a list of all the shop owners, all the entrepreneurs, all the professional people in our city who paid protection money, how much they paid and to whom. On the basis of this, the investigators had created an official map showing who controlled which part of the city.

Il Pizzo, "the Lace," is the term used for sums extorted from citizens for protection. Minimal in comparison to drug money, the Lace nevertheless plays a vital role as a sort of petty cash account for the Mafia, and also as a way of asserting control over territory through the criminal equivalent of taxes. According to Mafia informants, it is used to pay lawyers for arrested members and to give a "salary" to families whose men are in prison or have been killed, thus permitting Cosa Nostra to fund a criminal version of social security and enforce its code of *omertà*. Needless to say, anyone who refuses to buy into this scheme will have his shop or business damaged or might even pay with his life as an object lesson.

A brave man named Libero Grassi was to become such an object lesson a year after Falcone showed me the map. Grassi had a small business in a Mafia-saturated area in Palermo. He not only refused the pressing demands of the local boss, but agreed to appear on television where, looking straight at the camera, he almost spelled out the words: "Mafiosi, I will not pay!" Grassi also appealed to all the other businessmen of his area to follow his example, reminding them that if they *all* held firm, if they *all* stood united in their refusal to pay, the Mafia would be powerless, and they themselves would be less at risk. Early one morning as he went to buy his daily newspaper a few steps from his house, one of Cosa Nostra's killers shot Grassi in the head.

The map Giovanni Falcone had shown me the year before was an x-ray of the city's protection racket. Almost everybody paid—not great sums, perhaps, but enough to make it clear to everyone who was in control. One of the things Falcone pointed out to me was how little certain important and successful businessmen paid in proportion to their income. This meant that they were on the side of the victorious bosses. Another businessman, owner of a far smaller enterprise, paid a *huge* sum. This indicated that he had dared to support the losing faction or that he was unhappy about paying his protection money and let the collector know it. Through careful study of who paid how much to whom, a chilling picture of the city emerged. I was in a subdued mood when Falcone cut off our discussion for a meeting with Giulio Andreotti.

Andreotti had yet again become prime minister—for the seventh time. He was in Palermo to see Salvo Lima and his other friends and followers. But he had other business as well. The accomplishments of the Palermo Spring couldn't have meant less to him; he and his faction had been waiting for the smoke to clear from the Maxitrial to settle accounts. Andreotti began with a snide reference to the work of my friend Father Pintacuda when he was asked about the work of the City of Man organization: "Let the priests take care of our souls. The Lord has given us the grace of the state." Then, at a meeting of the provincial committee of the Christian Democratic Party, he got to the work at hand: a resolution was passed condemning my work and my "anomalous" coalition government.

It had been hard enough to govern over the last months, but with this development I realized it would now be impossible. I handed in my resignation, which was immediately accepted. Thousands of students, joined by ordinary citizens of all ages, marched through the streets and jammed Piazza Pretoria and all the nearby squares, roads and alleys. In spite of persistent rain—the Palermitan, like the cat, doesn't enjoy rain—they remained under the windows of Palazzo delle Aquile, shouting slogans and then jumping up and down on the spot, chanting: "He who doesn't jump is son of Andreotti!"

I too went down into the square. As soon as the people saw me, they set up a roar, and someone grabbed me by the hand and pulled me into their midst. I am neither especially fit nor especially lithe, but I too began to jump: "He who doesn't jump is son of Andreotti!"

My resignation took effect in March. There would be new elections then, and I made it clear that I intended to be a candidate again.

The intervening weeks were filled with political maneuvering, but when I look back at that time I remember an incident that had nothing to do with elections. A theft had occurred in the parish church of a district called Acquasanta. The ancient silver crown of the Madonna of Acquasanta had been taken—by a gypsy, it was said.

Because its history builds on many peoples of different races, cultures and religions, Palermo, in spite of all its violence, has an antiracist soul. The unemployed may have said "Long live the Mafia" or learned, during the Palermo Spring, to say "We want work from the state, not from the Mafia." But never once, in all the years I've been mayor, has one of these unemployed said to me: "It's not right that he, an African, has work while I don't"—something one unfortunately hears all too often in the rich north of Italy. There had been some minor problems in the past with Palermo's resident Romany, which my administration had settled, and I had given the head of the gypsy community my home telephone number as a way of keeping a line of communication open.

When I learned of the stolen crown of the Madonna of Acquasanta, I immediately contacted the Romany leader and let him know I considered the theft offensive to the history and beliefs of the people of Palermo. I heard nothing from him for weeks. Then on the day in March that I was to leave office, he finally called.

"You're still mayor?"

I told him that technically I was.

"Good. I must see you immediately."

We met at Villa Niscemi, where he opened a paper bag and handed me the silver crown. He told me that he had sent a request for help out to all the Romany communities in Italy. As it turned out, the crown had been stolen by a gypsy of the Florentine community and the thief had been apprehended on the Italian-French border by some of his own people. If Palermo's Romany leader had not intervened, the crown would undoubtedly have gone to enrich some antique dealer abroad, as so many of our art and archaeological treasures do. So my defeat that day turned into a victory: in a packed church, I returned the Madonna's crown to the parish priest, who had set the bells pealing to summon the local inhabitants to the church to hear a gypsy leader give a speech.

| | |

On the eve of the elections in March, Andreotti appeared on television to say, in his usual silky way, that if he were permitted to cast a vote in Palermo, he would choose from number two down on the Christian Democrat list. I, of course, was number one. But in spite of this condemnation by the most powerful man in the party and the country, I got more votes than any mayoral candidate had ever before received. My support came not only from my own party, but also from people who had never before voted Christian Democrat. The result was an irony: the Christian Democrats had a majority in the city council for the first time.

The party was embarrassed by my victory, but given its proportions, there was no way the party could designate anyone else as mayor. But they could and did insist that I form my government exclusively from members of my own party. No more of this "anomalous" governing with a handful of Greens and Communists thrown into the mix. For me to accept this diktat would have meant repudiating the achievements of the Palermo Spring, which had occurred despite rather than because of the Christian Democrats, and was based on mobilizing a large number of feuding groups who began to see that they had a larger kinship in the renewal of our city.

If I refused to become mayor, on the other hand, I would be accused of giving up the commitment to cleanse the Christian Democratic Party and in some way betraying the ghost of Piersanti Mattarella, for whom that had been the great goal. Yet that ghost and all the other ghosts of the illustrious corpses of the last ten years had been created both by shadowy Mafiosi who pulled triggers and placed car bombs, and by shadowy politicians operating not from hideouts but from the political institutions of our country. I decided to refuse the job as a way of making a statement about the symbiosis between the Mafia bosses and the political bosses.

| | |

The mayor of Trento, a city in the north of Italy, was a good political friend of mine also interested in the fight to liberate Palermo from the Mafia. It occurred to us to hold a meeting in his city and invite others who were sick of the reign of the Christian Democrats and interested in renewing the political system. A leading Italian newspaper picked up the news and headlined its story: "Orlando's Network to Meet in Trento." The Italian word for "network" is *la rete*. The term stuck and eventually became the name of our movement.

Before the meeting, I withdrew to a house I own in the small mountain village of Sauris, practically on the border between Italy and Austria. I wanted to write down some thoughts about a new kind of politics which I thought might succeed in Italy. La Rete would be a movement based on our fight against the Mafia, using that fight as a rallying point for those who believed, as we did, that the national political scene was filled with dry rot.

As I finished writing a draft of our manifesto, a breeze came through the open window and scattered my notes on the floor. This seemed appropriate because the movement I envisioned would have an end as well as a beginning. La Rete would last only for the time required to begin to change the conscience of Italy, and then it would end. It would not be a political party whose continued existence would cause compromise and contamination. And indeed, on March 21, 1991, the formal birth date of the movement, we filed the name with a notary in Rome, along with a statement beginning, "La Rete is a political movement with a limited lifespan."

The choice of March 21 was deliberate. This date marks the beginning of spring and I wanted the country to remember that the roots of La Rete were in the Palermo Spring. But it also grew from my personal history as a Sicilian Christian Democrat who was leaving the party, in my experience as a southerner who had shaken off the yoke of the Mafia, in my experience as a politician who believed that the sickness of party and crime in Sicily had contaminated the entire country.

Among the other founding members of La Rete were Alfredo Galasso, the prominent attorney who had represented the Dalla Chiesa family at the Maxitrial and who had never in his career defended Mafiosi. There was Nando Dalla Chiesa, son of the murdered general, who was a professor of sociology at a prestigious university in Milan, but had found himself spending more and more time in Sicily. There was Diego Novelli, former Communist mayor of Turin, who also left his party because he believed it was no longer committed to the battle against the Mafia and its corruption. There was Carlo Palermo (not a Sicilian, despite his name), a prosecutor in Trento whose investigations into drug and arms trafficking had led him to disquieting discoveries involving Italian politicians, especially from the Socialist Party, which at that time was headed by

Prime Minister Bettino Craxi. Harassed by the Socialists, Carlo had applied for a transfer to Trapani in Sicily to continue his investigations, but not long after his arrival a bomb exploded as his armored car was taking him to his office. He and his bodyguards survived, but a woman who happened to be driving past at that very moment was hit by the full force of the blast and was blown to pieces along with her twin little boys sitting in the back seat of her car.

With us of course was Father Ennio Pintacuda, who, being a priest, could not be formally among the founders of La Rete, but was there as a counselor and guiding spirit. Since 1980, through all the important events of my political life, Father Pintacuda had been at my side. He was one of those people who knows that the good fight is almost always a long fight.

Father Pintacuda's presence was symbolic, for La Rete was the first movement with the potential to split Italy's Catholic faithful away from the Christian Democratic Party, which had been their secular faith since World War II. Yet the "objective conditions," as my Communist friends liked to say, were changing in Italy. The Christian Democrats had watched the fall of the Berlin Wall and seen their own mortality. They had been in power for almost a half-century because they were one of the West's strongest bulwarks against communism and because the people in Italy who feared even a tepid Eurocommunism had no alternative. But in that time the CDs had become drunk on their own impunity and had disgusted people of strong moral beliefs. Now that the Cold War had ended, they were becoming unnecessary as well as unloved.

La Rete groups began springing up all over the country, self-financed, self-run, without a handful of wealthy financial backers pulling the strings. They existed only because of a small army of volunteers: young people, elderly people, professional women and housewives, angry men who felt betrayed, old pensioners whose souls shouted "Basta!"

The national press had paid great attention to all I said and did when I was working from within the Christian Democratic Party.

Now it lost interest in me. But the international press, which saw in La Rete the first sign of something new in Italian politics since the postwar period, gave us enormous coverage. Andrea Scrosati, La Rete's young press officer, learned that when we wanted notice for something we considered important, he should leak it to a foreign journalist, and when the item then appeared in prestigious foreign newspapers, the Italian press would be forced to pick it up.

The first elections in which La Rete was to be put to the test were regional elections for the Sicilian parliament held late in the spring of 1991. The experts all predicted that at most, I myself might be elected, at which point, being alone, I would either have to return to the Christian Democrat mother-house or join some other established party. We worked day and night, touring Sicily along with our supporters, with the result that not only was I elected, but La Rete carried five *Retini* (as the press had dubbed members of the movement) into Palazzo dei Normanni, the Norman Palace which was the seat of the oldest parliament in the world and now seat of the Sicilian regional parliament.

Soon after this victory I went to the United States for a long-planned visit. It began with a comedy of errors. Andrea Scrosati, working now as my spokesman, went ahead of me to arrange some briefings with American newspapers. Traveling under an assumed name, as always, I arrived but was not met at the plane because the Italian government, still dominated by Christian Democrats, was treating me as a nonperson. Because the United States was at that time the second largest Mafia country after Sicily, Andrea became concerned when I didn't show up at the hotel. He called the New York police, but when he told them about who I was and about the assumed name, they thought he was perpetrating a hoax. Andrea became so desperate that he started calling all the U.S. phone numbers he had. Finally, he found someone who recognized my name because he had seen a *60 Minutes* segment about me, and he authenticated the story with the police. A protective detail was immediately arranged by the NYPD to follow me all the time I was in town.

On this trip I talked to several major media organizations. I talked about Sicily and its political sickness. I also gave my views on how the Mafia was becoming an international phenomenon, not just a Sicilian or even an American one. This would soon become common knowledge, but at the time of my visit it was seen as something new. When I predicted that Mafia-like organizations would soon crop up in the former Soviet Union and other countries, a reporter from *USA Today* called the FBI, which confirmed what I was saying. The *USA Today* headline read, "Italian Politician Predicts That Mafia Will Arrive from Russia." The story was then picked up by the *New York Times*, CNN, and others.

When I returned home, I was denounced by people in the Ministry of Foreign Affairs for speaking ill of my country. Yet what I said had an even bigger impact than they realized. Years later, when Giulio Andreotti was being called to account for the connection between the Mafia and his Christian Democrats, someone asked him when his troubles began, I was told, and Andreotti replied that part of his difficulty started in 1991 because of my visit to the United States.

| | |

At the same time as La Rete was making its first appearance on the national political scene, Giovanni Falcone finally left Palermo. Embittered and frustrated, he had decided to take the job of director of penal affairs at the Ministry of Justice in Rome. Since the day he had been passed over by the Superior Council of Magistrates, his life in Palermo had been a succession of humiliations. The truce called between the pro- and anti-Falcone forces in the summer of 1988 had made the animosities less public but no less lacerating. Falcone had tried to find some way of continuing his antimafia work in Sicily, but finally had to admit that he had been stalemated. Yet he didn't want to give up trying to build a system that could give law enforcement officials more power in their fight against organized crime. He began contacting government figures in Rome to see if there was a place for his ideas on the national scene.

Many of us in Sicily—myself included—were skeptical. We feared that Falcone might be exploited by politicians in Rome who were covertly connected to the Mafia. And so when he left to take a new job there, he did it against the advice of most of his friends, including Paolo Borsellino. The two men had always been tied by a strong bond, almost as if they knew it was their fate eventually to become a single hyphenated name. Yet now Paolo opposed Falcone's decision because he thought his friend would be dead-ended in a bureaucratic job, and even more because he thought it was wrong to join an administration headed by Andreotti. Paolo was very much aware of Falcone's flaw, which, as in all tragic heroes, was the flaw of pride—in this case a prideful belief that he could solve all our problems from the inside. Falcone replied that the minister of justice who had offered him the job, the Socialist Claudio Martelli, really wanted to make changes. With that single-mindedness which was both his virtue and his vice, he left for Rome in March of 1991.

As it worked out, those of us who criticized him did not sufficiently appreciate Falcone's plan in taking the new job. He knew from experience just how serious a drawback the fragmented judicial system was in dealing with Mafia investigations, particularly when put against the unity of Cosa Nostra. He immediately began to interrogate judges throughout the country with an eye to finding what they knew of Mafia activities. Just as the Antimafia Pool in Palermo had succeeded by sharing information, so Italy as a whole, he believed, would be aided by a similar national pooling of investigative data on the Mafia. This had not happened in the past. Each regional and city office held its information tightly—information that might perhaps hide the key to some colleague's investigations—unless there happened to be a personal relationship between magistrates. So Falcone decided to fight for what the press would later call a *Superprocura Antimafia*, a national antimafia prosecutor's office which would coordinate information from investigations of Mafia activities.

It was time to think of the next step. The verdicts of the Maxitrial had slowly made their way through the Appeals Court and although the sentencing had been reduced for some of the defendants, it had not been the debacle that some of us feared. Now the Mafia's only hope lay in the Supreme Court. Cosa Nostra could feel a certain confidence here. Over the years, the president of the First Section of the court, Judge Corrado Carnevale, who would get the case if something was not done, had become known as the "sentence killer" because of his record in throwing out guilty verdicts in Mafia cases. As one prosecutor in the Palermo Pool had once put it when speaking with me about the Supreme Court: "We magistrates are but human and we can all make mistakes… but it's not possible that we are all *always* wrong. It's just not possible!"

La Rete began to pressure the president of the Republic and the Superior Council of Magistrates to observe the principle of rotation and let others preside over the First Section of the court. Our fears increased when, in August 1991, Judge Antonio Scopelliti was killed while on holiday in Calabria. The stern Scopelliti, with a reputation for being "unapproachable," had just been appointed public prosecutor for the Supreme Court case of the Maxitrial. The murder was intended as a warning. But as before, this act of violence boomeranged on Cosa Nostra.

On January 31, 1992, the First Section of the Supreme Court in Rome, no longer headed by Judge Carnevale, announced its historic verdict upholding the life sentences and the hundreds of years of imprisonment meted out in the previous two trials. But even more important, the court confirmed the principle that Cosa Nostra was not just a collection of single criminals, but a criminal association bound by hierarchy, rules and joint interests.

A line had been crossed. We would later learn from another Mafia informer named Gaspare Mutolo that once the Supreme Court decision was announced, low-level Mafiosi with outstanding warrants began giving themselves up by the dozens. This was the only way they knew of rebelling against Riina, whom they regarded as a psychotic who had destroyed the invisibility that they and their kind had always relied upon. It was also a way of getting out of the path of the Götterdämmerung they knew was coming.

| | |

La Rete rejoiced at the Supreme Court's verdict. We were in the middle of our first national electoral campaign, for elections that would take place in spring. A bizarre backdrop for these elections was established two weeks after the Supreme Court verdict, when a small-time functionary in the Socialist Party named Mario Chiesa was arrested in Milan, caught red-handed as he was accepting a $7,000 bribe. This turned out to be the Italian equivalent of the Watergate break-in. As Chiesa was interviewed, he admitted that he had $10 million in bribe money stashed in Swiss banks. Prosecutors in Milan's prosecutor's office soon formed a pool of their own, the "Clean Hands Pool." As they probed what initially appeared to be a minor crime, they began to uncover a system of bribery and corruption that stretched to the top of Italian financial and political circles. Socialist leader Bettino Craxi and the political machine he had built were deeply implicated, but so were the Christian Democrats.

The Chiesa arrest began a saga that paralleled the efforts of the antimafia in Sicily. In the next two years we were to see one after another of the country's most powerful men being accused of accepting bribes and kickbacks and at times of extorting monies for their parties or themselves. And we were to discover that just about all companies, big or small, who had contracts with local or national administrations paid a fixed percentage in kickbacks. Italian citizens learned how all public works had cost the taxpayer two or three times what they should have cost, how millions of dollars had gone into private pockets to the detriment of the public health service, how the cost of services had been higher than it should have been because of this rotten political system. We were to see on national television one politician after another stutter "I don't recall" or "I have forgotten" as they were questioned in court.

This investigation would ultimately bring about the death of the Christian Democratic Party, which split into half a dozen little political parties, and the almost total disappearance of the Socialist Party, as its all-powerful leader Craxi retired to his villa in Tunisia, where he declared himself an exile who had been "persecuted" by Italian law.

Although this was still in the future, the whole system was beginning to creak. With the new insights into corruption, and with the collapse of the Soviet empire, the rationale for national power arrangements that had secretly embraced and legitimated the Mafia was gone. I saw a real possibility for La Rete to step into the political vacuum being created by these intimations of corruption. I toured the country continuously, from north to south, campaigning in squares, parish halls and student centers. The feeling that we were gaining support was confirmed when I was asked to appear on national television on March 12 for the first time in my role as national secretary of La Rete. But that evening there was no chance to speak about our movement. All questions focused on another death in Palermo.

At 8:30 that morning, Salvo Lima, member of the European Parliament and long-time fixer for the Christian Democrats in Sicily, left his villa in Mondello with a friend to do some campaigning. He had plenty of people to see, especially since his own political boss, Giulio Andreotti, was scheduled to visit Sicily in a few days. Lima's car hadn't yet picked up speed when two men on a motorcycle overtook them. The man on the back pulled out a pistol and shot out the tires. As the car came to a stop, the motorcyclists, their faces obscured by the visors on their helmets, turned purposefully back. Both Lima and the other man jumped out and began running for their lives, but the killers bore down on them and, pointedly ignoring the terrified friend cowering behind a trash trolley, emptied a revolver into Lima's face and chest and within seconds were off.

This was a seismic shift from the killings of lawmen and politicians who had opposed the Mafia. Lima was not only the kingmaker of an entire region and a member of the European Parliament to boot; he was also a friend of the Mafia. This killing was Cosa Nostra's response to the Supreme Court decision, a reaction to what it regarded as the Christian Democrats' breach of contract. The politicians with whom they had been in alliance all those years had either decided to withdraw that protection, or no longer had the power to make good on their guarantee. As *pentito* Gaspare Mutolo later said, Lima was a "maximum symbol" of those who had received Cosa Nostra votes but "no longer protected its interests at the precise moment of its most important trial."

Lima's murder was a sign that the tenuous status quo had ruptured. Now anything could happen.

That night on television I would have liked to speak of the cultural development of Italy, of the future envisioned by La Rete, but I had to acknowledge that such things were possible only if Italy was liberated from the plague that had settled down upon it. I condemned the brutal murder, but reminded my interviewers that this man had been a guarantor of a political-Mafioso system. A couple of days later, a gray-faced Giulio Andreotti was in the front pew at Salvo Lima's funeral. Paolo Borsellino commented that the Mafia had in effect laid Lima's body as a calling card on Andreotti's doorstep. And indeed, police picked up rumors that Andreotti's son had also been targeted for murder.

| | |

At the April 1992 national elections, La Rete sent twelve deputies to Parliament and three senators to the Senate. It was regarded as a stunning debut in a country where capturing 2 or 3 percent of the vote is considered significant.

I felt that we were living a season of signs and wonders. Although I am no great fan of the Book of Revelation, it seemed to me that the seventh seal could open at any time.

10

On May 23, 1992, La Rete was holding a meeting in Assisi, the beautiful Umbrian medieval city where St. Francis was born, and where the narrow streets continue to emanate his message of serenity and peace. We had not yet begun our session when I got a phone call from my personal secretary in Palermo, saying that a bomb had just exploded somewhere on the highway between Punta Raisi Airport and the city. He was speaking from his small holiday house at Capaci, a seaside resort where he and his wife had gone for the weekend, and he had heard the explosion. There was still no official word, but he had caught rumors that perhaps the car of a prosecutor had been involved in the blast. I asked him to keep me informed, and then began the meeting with a deep sense of foreboding.

A few minutes later, a police officer entered the hall and gestured to me. I quickly closed the meeting and asked him what was happening. He told me the horrible news: A hit squad of Mafia soldiers had planted a bomb near the Capaci turnoff. Giovanni Falcone, his wife, Francesca Morvillo, and three of Falcone's bodyguards had been killed in an explosion which had blown an enormous crater in the highway near the Capaci exit.

I rushed to Rome and remained there overnight, talking on the phone and at the same time watching the horrifying pictures on television—the twisted metal that had once been automobiles; the crater that looked like it had been created by a military aircraft; the information that Falcone had died immediately but Francesca had made it to the hospital, where she had revived long enough to ask "Where's Giovanni?" and then died on the operating table. I thought about the progress Falcone had made in Rome: setting up a super-prosecutor for the Mafia, establishing an Italian equivalent of the FBI, removing the judicial roadblocks that would have prevented the Supreme Court verdict. His insistence on going to Rome against the advice of all his friends had paid off. He had become a scourge of the Mafia there far more than he had ever been in Palermo, just as he promised. And now the promise he had come to represent lay buried in the debris of that explosion.

For the Mafia and the politicians linked to it, Falcone's murder was more than the elimination of an enemy. It was also the destruc-tion of a symbol. And symbols must be destroyed in a symbolic way. Falcone could far more easily have been killed in Rome, where he had come to enjoy a certain amount of freedom over the past few months, inviting friends to his apartment (there had been cham-pagne toasts on the night of the Supreme Court verdict and a vic-tory call to Borsellino and others in Sicily), occasionally escaping with Francesca to enjoy a quiet dinner and even a movie. But the Mafia needed to reaffirm its strength after so many defeats. In hit-ting Giovanni Falcone, the primary symbol of the antimafia in Sicily, Cosa Nostra was showing that it, not the state, was in control.

In time, all the details of that massacre became known. Three hundred kilos of explosive had been placed in a small drainage tun-nel running under the highway on which Falcone's motorcade was obliged to pass on its way from the airport to Palermo, where he nearly always returned on weekends. (But normally he returned on Friday evening, not Saturday. Who had alerted them to his change of plan?) Falcone and his wife had arrived on a security plane and immediately climbed into the cars waiting for him on the tarmac. Also waiting was a member of the Mafia commando, already tipped off by a contact at Da Vinci Airport in Rome, who used a cell phone to advise the hit team exactly when the motorcade left the airport.

What nobody knew was that because Francesca tended to become carsick in the armored Fiat, she chose to sit in the front, and Falcone, who always wished to be beside her, decided to drive. The usual driver got into the back.

Cosa Nostra's death squad had worked everything out to the split second. They deposited the wreck of an old refrigerator at the side of the highway to use as a marker for when to push the button on the explosive packed under the highway by men dressed as road workers. They rehearsed with speeding cars so as to calculate precisely when to trigger the detonator. Then they waited on a hill overlooking a clear stretch of the highway, having lopped off the top branches of some olive trees near the road to get a better view.

Falcone's driver, Giuseppe Costanzo, who miraculously emerged from the blast alive, said afterward that as they were speeding along, he asked Falcone, "Dottore, will you be needing the car again today?"

"No," answered Falcone, "I'll see you tomorrow."

"Well then, Dottore, when we arrive, don't forget that that's my key in the ignition."

Falcone then did something "completely crazy," as Costanzo put it. He suddenly pulled out the key and turned, as if to give it to him.

"For God's sake, Dottore, what are you doing? You'll kill us all!"

Because of Falcone's uncharacteristic jest, the car had slowed suddenly as it was passing the roadside refrigerator, and thus fell a few meters behind the bombers' calculations. The full blast, intended to hit Falcone's car from directly underneath, the only vulnerable part of an armored car, struck the leading car with three bodyguards and the front half of Falcone's car. The driver remembered nothing else. He woke up in the hospital, psychologically shattered and physically maimed but alive.

The entire Italian nation was stunned. For the previous ten days, members of Parliament and the Senate had jointly been trying to elect the new president of the Republic, Cossiga's term having expired. The result had been a stalemate of vetoes and counter-vetoes on the various names suggested, leaving the disenchanted nation with an impression of pettiness and impotence. "Operation Clean Hands" had begun to lift the lid off the cesspit of corruption in the north, and the stench was already overpowering. The day after Falcone's assassination, Piazza Montecitorio, the large square in front of the Parliament in Rome, was full of demonstrators angered by the murder of a national hero and the political degeneracy that had allowed it to happen.

That Monday morning, the people of Palermo once again gathered around the Church of San Domenico, just as they had done almost exactly ten years earlier for the funeral of Carlo Alberto Dalla Chiesa. This time it was Falcone, his wife and his three bodyguards being laid to rest. As before, the air was filled with tension as the few politicians who dared to brave the crowd's vituperation quickly scuttled through police cordons to take their places in the basilica. And just as ten years before, when the voice of Palermo's Cardinal Pappalardo had spoken out in accusation, so this time the voice of another Sicilian entered every Italian's home via radio and television. It was Rosaria Schifani, the stunning twenty-three-year-old widow of one of Falcone's three protectors, who spoke her despairing words in front of the altar.

Slender, with long black hair, a beautiful face and large dark eyes, Rosaria looked like a sorrowing Sicilian Madonna as she spoke the word "state" in her eulogy for her dead husband, then repeated it again with infinite contempt and despair: "In the name of all those who have given their lives for the state... yes... the *state*... I ask above all... for justice.... Now... I appeal to the men of the Mafia... because they *are* in here... but are certainly not Christians... you must know... that for you too there is the possibility of forgiveness.... I forgive you... but you must get down on your knees!"

Falcone's old boss, Antonino Caponnetto, and his friend Paolo Borsellino stood together like father and son, Caponnetto gazing at the coffins with brimming eyes, Borsellino standing there with a wrathful look on his face. Nando Dalla Chiesa and I, both newly elected members of the national Parliament, decided not to join the authorities inside the church but instead remained outside in the midst of the crowd of shocked citizens. At the end of the funeral, we flew to Rome, where that same day the Parliament and the Senate jointly elected Oscar Luigi Scalfaro as Italy's ninth president of the Republic. The next day, before being sworn in, Scalfaro decided to come to Palermo to pay homage to Giovanni Falcone, Francesca Morvillo and the three bodyguards. He asked that I be there beside him.

The people of Palermo were reacting as they had never reacted before, with women taking the lead. For any Sicilian woman, particularly a housewife, bed sheets represent something intimate and very private. Now sheets were appearing on balconies all over the city, with slogans painted on in red, as if with Falcone's blood: "Down with the Mafia!" "Truth and justice!" and "Falcone lives!" The "Committee of the Sheets" had been born.

These white flags were not calling for a truce, but for retribution. They meant that the family in that house—whose neighbor might be directly or indirectly tied to the Mafia—was not afraid to indicate publicly which side of the barricade it stood on. At first the sheets were few and far between, but as the days passed, they multiplied—even in Mafia strongholds like Brancaccio where it took a lot of guts to proclaim one's convictions. And when the women of the sheets marched in demonstrations, shouting up toward shuttered windows, sometimes one of them would open a crack and a woman's hand would suddenly shake out a tablecloth or napkin or something else, and then withdraw it. The message was clear: the woman inside, though not permitted by her man to hang out a sheet, was finding a way to express solidarity nonetheless.

Right beside the entrance door of the block of flats where Falcone lived stands an enormous banyan tree. The street is Notarbartolo, named after banker Emanuele Notarbartolo, whose murder in 1893 made him the first of Sicily's illustrious corpses. Once again, totally spontaneously, people began to bring flowers which they placed at the foot of this tree, and with the flowers some of them left a little note or a poem or some words with a photo, which they pinned to the tree trunk: "Thank you Giovanni." "We will continue your fight." "We shall not forget Giovanni, Francesca, Vito, Antonio and Rocco." Every note there had a signature: anonymous disapproval of the Mafia was no longer acceptable.

Then someone pinned a page on the tree saying: TODAY BEGINS A DAWN THAT WILL SEE NO SUNSET. It was so different from the despair in the sign that went up after Dalla Chiesa's assassination ten years before: "Here dies the hope of honest Palermitans."

This banyan tree has become known as *L'albero di Falcone*, "Falcone's Tree," and today it is still a site of pilgrimage.

| | |

On the morning of June 23, a month after the Capaci attack, a human chain formed across Palermo, stretching symbolically from the prosecutor's office through the central streets of the city to Falcone's Tree. Thousands of people joined hands in silent testimony of their determination not to forget and, more important, to make sure that the Mafia knew they were now, after all the years of civic preparation, a force to be reckoned with.

Two days later, in the evening, there was to be a debate in the arched courtyard of the municipal library, which was attached to the Church of Casa Professa where I used to meet with Father Ennio Pintacuda and other Gonzaga alumni so many years before, when the Mafia was a word we were just learning to use. Several people were scheduled to speak: Nando Dalla Chiesa, Father Pintacuda, myself and some others. But all eyes in the overcrowded courtyard that night were on Paolo Borsellino. He had been back in the prosecutor's office in Palermo for the past few months, having returned after being given a guarantee that he would be permitted to continue his investigations into the Mafia, particularly in the provinces of Agrigento and Trapani, which he now knew better than anyone else. He had always worked obsessively. But after Falcone's death, as both his family and colleagues were later to confirm, there was a feverish quality in his work, as if he knew that he had to burn white-hot because his time was running out.

He arrived late and the debate had already started, but as he entered, surrounded by his numerous bodyguards, applause began and accompanied him as he took his place. In that applause was the acknowledgment that with Falcone's death, Borsellino had moved up to the head of the Mafia's most-wanted list. (It would later emerge that Paolo had told his family long ago, "First they will kill Giovanni and then they will kill me.") On this evening, he spoke without any notes. Always eloquent, he reached a new level in creating what many of those present would recall as the most significant public moment they had experienced. Paolo did not say much about the fact that he had personally been investigating his friend's death; nor did he mention that there had been some discussions about his going to Rome to take on the job of super-prosecutor of the Mafia, which Falcone had designed. He spoke with intensity, anger and sorrow as he traced the last difficult years of Giovanni's career and life, almost hypnotically tapping his cigarette lighter on the table as he spoke of "those Judases" among his colleagues who had betrayed Falcone. Again and again he was interrupted by applause and many in the rapt audience were weeping. When he finished speaking, everybody jumped up and gave him a standing ovation that wouldn't let him go. I had an almost choking sensation—as many others also later reported—so certain was I that this wild applause was a farewell to a man we all knew had been condemned to death. As he stood there looking out at the audience, Paolo had a look of strength and resolution on his face as if he knew it too.

| | |

The following week, I was in my tiny rented attic apartment in the heart of Rome, around the corner from the Pantheon and a few blocks away from Parliament. I had rented the place when I was elected to Parliament from La Rete and had come to love it immediately. One only had to go out the door to step into two thousand years of history and simultaneously be immersed in the life and vitality of the twentieth century. It was already late at night and I was just considering going to bed when my escort suddenly broke into the room.

"Quick! quick! You have to come with us immediately. The threat is imminent. There's no time to waste!"

With nothing but the clothes I was wearing, I was hustled out to a squad car that sped off to a police barracks.

They had received reliable information that the order had gone out to kill Borsellino and Orlando, and they believed there was going to be a bomb attack against me right there in the historical center of Rome. I was never again allowed to set foot in my wonderful apartment. For the rest of the time I was a member of Parliament, my home was the police barracks where I had been taken that night.

And so began the nerve-racking wait to see who was next and when. Paolo and I spoke several times a week on the phone. Each time it was with great affection, almost sentimentality, neither of us knowing if there would be another conversation. We had been warned to speak in code on matters involving security issues, but Paolo sometimes got carried away and ignored these instructions. As he did the last time we spoke. I had called him on his cell phone on a Sunday because I needed to arrange a meeting with him. He answered: "I'm on the highway to Punta Raisi…. I'm going to Germany…. When I get back I'll call you and we'll meet up."

"Paolo!" I tried to interrupt him. "I don't want to know where you're going and I don't want to know when you're coming back! Just call me when you can."

Two weeks later I was in Vibo Valenzia, a town in the southern region of Calabria. We had just finished a two-day assembly for all the offices of La Rete in that region, part of an effort to build up and strengthen this movement. Because of the Calabrese variant of the Mafia called 'Ndrangheta, La Rete faced a difficult task in its attempts to stir consciences and get civil society to react to a political system as corrupt as Sicily's. I was back in my hotel when the chief of police appeared and brusquely said to me:

"You can't move from here. We've this minute been informed of a bomb attack in Palermo."

Nothing else. No information on where, who. I was taken to my room and told to lock myself in while a dozen or so policemen stationed themselves in the corridor. The first news I got described a huge cloud of black smoke in the area of my home. A few minutes later the locale had shifted to the area where prosecutor Giuseppe Ayala lived. With my heart in my mouth I called home.

"Milli, for God's sake, what's happened?" I was relieved to hear her voice.

She told me that she had been in her car when she heard this massive explosion, apparently coming from the direction of Via d'Amelio. And then, shortly after hanging up, I got definitive word. It was Paolo.

For the rest of my life, that afternoon and night will remain a nightmare. I asked to be able to go immediately to Palermo and was told that I could go nowhere. Even if they wanted to, the police didn't know how to get me out of Vibo Valenzia because they'd received warning that there was a car bomb on the road to Lamezia Terme, the closest airport. So I remained there for hours, imprisoned in my hotel room. All broadcasting had been interrupted and one of the RAI national television channels was transmitting the horror of burnt cars, flames, dense black smoke, shattered windows for six stories, blood everywhere, staggering firemen with blackened faces and bodies, and pieces of bodies covered with sheets. It was Dante's hell.

After several hours somebody decided to send out a motorcade, including my car but without me in it. It set off, blue lights flashing and sirens screaming, and information was leaked that I was on my way to Bari on the Adriatic coast. Then, with any hit squads hopefully misled, a police helicopter landed in front of the hotel a short time later and I was spirited off to the airport. There, once again I was locked into a room. I was told that an undersecretary from the Ministry of the Interior had arrived and wished to meet me to ask how I was. The hours of tension, the horror of those images still filling my eyes, suddenly made me crack. I began shouting that I would see nobody, that I wanted to go to Palermo. But then, having let off some of the tension, I talked to the undersecretary. Together we explored possible ways of getting me secretly out of Lamezia. Finally at midnight, I was hustled onto a mail plane. Surrounded by packages and bags of letters I arrived in Rome, where I was immediately taken to my lodgings in the police barracks.

At last I found out exactly what had happened when the next installment of the Apocalypse hit Palermo that Sunday afternoon, leaving six victims dead on the Via d'Amelio, with many more wounded by splintered glass and falling debris, and over a hundred people evacuated from their homes after the explosion.

In his last few weeks, Paolo had often said, "I have no time for what I have to do." Those who knew him well understood that he was talking about mortality, not his caseload. He no longer tolerated his lack of freedom and kept disappearing, jumping into his own car and eluding his bodyguard to drive through the city. The Ministry of Justice had tried to stop him. He had told them, You let me do this or I'll accuse you of kidnapping, and he meant it.

That morning Borsellino had been in his place in Villagrazia di Carini, a seaside resort between Capaci and the airport. After lunch he had called his mother on what he thought was a secure line to say he would be at her home around five o'clock for a quick visit. Cosa Nostra was tapping her phone. When his cars arrived, his five bodyguards jumped out, submachine guns at the ready, searching the windows of the tall apartment blocks but for some reason not noticing the car parked in front of the building. Paolo quickly got out and with his left hand buzzed the intercom. In his right he held his last cigarette.

His murder occurred in the usual cloud of unknowing. Why had the area in front of his mother's house not been declared a "no parking" zone, as requested weeks earlier? Why had he gone to

Germany a few days before his death? Had he spoken to anybody about his latest investigations? What about the call he received at 7:30 that morning, while he was writing a letter of encouragement to a schoolteacher concerned about the world her students would inherit? It was one of his superiors telling him that Mutolo, the new *pentito* he had previously not been allowed to interview, would now be made available to him. Why not wait until the following morning, a Monday, to pass along this information? Was there an ulterior motive in that call?

In another country and another time, perhaps such questions would not be asked. But during the days of the Mafia's last offensive, suspicion was the antechamber of truth.

CHAPTER

11

How much sorrow and anger can a city bear? Giovanni Falcone was better known, in Italy and internationally, but Paolo Borsellino's death affected Palermo in a very profound way. He was essentially a common man, one whose unaffected manner, capacity for feeling, and even his way of speaking, with a marked Palermo accent, gave him a humanity that made his fellow citizens feel he was one of them. But he was also a person of extraordinary moral force, and he left his imprint on everyone he came in contact with. I am not alone in having felt a saintly quality in Borsellino.

One of Borsellino's daughters was on holiday in the Far East, and the family decided to postpone his funeral until her return. It would be held in the small parish church where he had gone to daily Mass, and the people of Palermo, respecting the privacy of the Borsellino family, did not congregate at the church but stood on the streets and solemnly applauded as the hearse drove by. Meanwhile, there was a service for four of Borsellino's bodyguards. (The family of the fifth, a young policewoman, in disgust refused to participate.) More than four thousand *carabinieri* were present, holding attack dogs and erecting crush barriers all around the cathedral to keep the people at a distance.

Nando Dalla Chiesa and I arrived at one of the barriers. Just as they were about to let us through, I heard shouts.

"They won't let us in! Orlando, Orlando… these are *our* dead! They've let in the Mafioso politicians and they're keeping us out!"

I asked an official why the people were not being allowed to pass.

"Orders," he answered, sweating profusely.

The mood was getting ugly. I told the official that we too would not enter as long as Palermo's citizens were kept out. Round the front of the cathedral we could hear that the barriers had been broken and a tide of people was rushing toward the door. The official made a small opening and we filed through.

The cathedral, packed to the bursting point with citizens, was also filled with silence during the celebration of the Mass. But afterward, as the coffins, covered with the Italian flag, were lifted to be carried out and the authorities began moving down the aisle, the pent-up anger exploded: "Jackals! Murderers!" "Buffoons!"

Shoving, spitting and punching greeted the national chief of police, who with panicked eyes nearly clung to President Scalfaro for protection. For a few moments anything might have happened, but then a wild-looking man with long, untidy grey hair and an unkempt white beard grabbed a microphone.

"Stay calm!" he implored. "I'm Agostino's father… I'm one of you! But we must stay calm and remain united!"

Agostino was a policeman who had been killed by the Mafia together with his twenty-year-old pregnant wife two years before, and the old man had sworn not to cut his hair or beard until the mysteries surrounding his son's death—mysteries that pointed at security involvement—were cleared up and justice was done. His desperate appeal restrained the violent feelings inside the cathedral and allowed the authorities to escape.

| | |

I was already scheduled to appear on the most important television talk show in Italy that evening, and I was at the Punta Raisi Airport boarding a private plane sent by the producer when I saw soldiers disembarking from a military transport. They were the first contingent of five thousand men the national government had decided to send to Sicily in a military operation called "Sicilian Vespers," the name coming from a thirteenth-century uprising of citizens in Palermo and Corleone against the French occupation. The army would control territory and protect strategic targets of the Mafia—the homes of magistrates, the Tribunal, my own home—thus permitting hundreds of policemen and *carabinieri*, up till then used simply as sentries, to return to their investigative and law enforcement activities.

When I got to Rome, the minister of the interior, no particular friend of mine, called to say that the security service had received information that I would be the next illustrious corpse. My spokesman, Andrea Scrosati, advised that increasing my visibility was the best defense.

A few hours later, I was sitting across from Maurizio Costanzo, the leading figure in Italian television journalism, on the darkened stage of the theater from which his show was broadcast. Costanzo always has several guests; this was the first show he had devoted to only one. He asked brief questions and allowed me to give long answers about the desperation, fear, and hope of all Sicilians. I knew I was marked for death and that this appearance offered me not only a chance to say what Paolo would have said about the forces of darkness covering our martyred land, but also an opportunity for survival. I looked directly into the cameras and said, "If I am killed, the assassins will be Mafiosi, but the orders will have come from the politicians."

At the end of the show, Costanzo asked me for closing remarks. Perhaps he was expecting some lofty words for his audience, who had sat through the interview in electrified silence. But some primal instinct made me look at the cameras and cry out: *"I want to live!"*

| | |

Falcone, Borsellino and Orlando—in that order. Later on, as the Mafia occupation of Palermo was finally being broken, a recently surfaced Mafia informer named Baldassare Di Maggio told investigators that Totò Riina, Cosa Nostra's boss of bosses, was infuriated by the Maxitrial verdict of the Supreme Court and had sworn revenge, demanding these three deaths. But seeing the nation's reaction to the murder of Borsellino, the Commission, supreme governing body of the Mafia, flatly vetoed Riina's insistence that a hit team proceed with the third killing—mine. According to Di Maggio, the Commission was distressed by the military occupation and even more by the fact that the Mafia was losing what little support it still had among the people. Moreover, the killing of Falcone and Borsellino had provoked such a strong reaction from the official world that a growing number of Mafiosi, seeing the handwriting on the wall, were meeting with magistrates and offering to turn state's witness. (From his Witness Protection haven in the United States, Tommaso Buscetta, who had always before refused to talk about the political dimension, said that to honor the memory of his great "fallen enemy" Giovanni Falcone, he was now finally prepared to tell what he knew of Cosa Nostra's political connections.) Killing me, the members of the provincial Commission told Riina, would be suicide.

I didn't know all this at the time, but every minute expected the explosion that would bring darkness. After Borsellino's death, I sent Milli and our daughters away from Palermo, having them assume false names which were continually changed as they stayed with friends, never in the same place longer than a few days at a time. Never once did I let Milli phone me as she moved from one town in Italy to another, for fear that the call would be traced. Eleonora and Leila were packed off to Greece, where they stayed incommunicado.

It was a lonely time, though I was never at home myself. I was either living in barracks, in Rome or Palermo, or touring the country under heavy guard. As far as possible, I tried to think of myself as someone already condemned and waiting only to discover the moment of execution. At times I was almost impatient, asking my unseen enemies, Why don't you just get on with it? What I didn't know was that having decided not to kill me physically, they were determined to kill me morally.

I found my achievements being turned back upon me. The fact that I had fought the Mafia with all the energy and determination of which I was capable, from *within* the Christian Democratic Party, became a bizarre accusation: "Orlando was a member of a party in collusion with the Mafia, and then he betrayed the Mafia." Articles were planted in the Italian press claiming that such-and-such an unnamed *pentito* was telling investigators that he'd heard that I'd had "contacts" with high-level Mafiosi. There was never any proof offered, of course, but this did not stop unnamed political figures—the people Giovanni Falcone had in mind when he spoke of "extremely refined minds which are attempting to guide certain actions of the Mafia"—from reviving the charge that I was an "anti-mafia professional." Nor did it stop the most painful charge of all: that I was guilty of being alive, of having survived while all the others had been killed.

| | |

Even in this grim time, there were moments of comic relief. A major German television network, ZDF, had a live show called *Menschen* which every year selected Men of the Year in various categories. Early in 1993 I was informed that I had been chosen European Politician of the Year and was invited to ZDF's gala in Berlin. Although the German police agency specializing in organized crime and terrorism considered Germany a high-risk country for people such as myself (the explosive for the Borsellino massacre apparently came from there), I accepted the invitation.

I was accompanied by Andrea Scrosati, who booked our flights under false names from a public phone. My protection abroad was always in the hands of local police authorities, which meant that Interpol had to inform its counterpart in whichever country I traveled of the time of my arrival.

At Rome Airport, the Alitalia plane left its dock and started to taxi toward the runway. At a certain point, the pilot stopped as I was driven up in an armored car. The irritated passengers all had to leave the plane and one by one re-identify their luggage, which was unloaded onto the tarmac. By the time we finally took off, we were over an hour late, which meant that by the time we landed in Frankfurt, we had missed our connecting flight. The German security service agent who met the plane told us there would be more than an hour's wait before the next flight. In an embarrassed tone, he told us that the only place for us was in the airport jail.

When we were put onto the next Lufthansa flight for Berlin, the same procedure was repeated. We boarded at the last minute, the passengers were made to disembark and claim their luggage, the plane itself was thoroughly checked, and of course, once again the flight was delayed. The Italian passengers had been patient, but the Germans, accustomed to Teutonic precision, made such a fuss that the captain came out of the cockpit and begged for their understanding. I must confess that I tried to make myself very small behind an open newspaper.

In Berlin we were once again met by security men and hustled into two different armored cars, a BMW and the official armored Mercedes used for foreign heads of state. There were also motorcyclists, and as we soon realized, at least a dozen unmarked police cars. For almost a full hour and a half we whizzed through the slow Berlin traffic at high speed. At one point we came to the hotel where we were supposed to be staying and drove straight past.

Almost at the last minute, we finally arrived at ZDF's studios, where I was able to change quickly in a dressing room before the show. After the ceremonies were completed, I was invited to the reception that the station had organized in a nearby beerhouse. My escort tried to prevent me from attending, but I insisted. I was tired, but I finally relaxed and began having a good time, and then my escort decided that we had to go. There was another mad, circuitous race through the city that lasted for well over an hour. Finally we arrived at our hotel—not the one where we had been booked, but another, in which German security had taken over a full floor. Stepping out of the elevator, we looked straight into the severe face of a military man holding a machine gun and standing behind sandbags.

Finally I demanded to know what was going on. I was told that despite all our precautions—calls from public telephone booths, false names—there must have been a leak, because a stolen car had been found parked right in front of the entrance to the hotel where we were originally booked.

There was an amusing little ending to that day of tension. Just as we were being escorted into the hotel chosen by the police, two men stepped out the front door. One stared at me a moment and then exclaimed to the other, in a broad Palermo accent: *"Miiii... il Sindaco Orlando è!"* "Hey!... it's Mayor Orlando!"

Poor fellows! They were pounced upon, questioned for hours, their rooms and belongings searched until everyone agreed that they were innocent tourists who happened to be in the wrong place at the wrong time. I don't think they soon forgot their visit to Berlin!

| | |

A few days later, along with Simona, one of General Dalla Chiesa's daughters, I was speaking to students at the University of Catanzaro, in Calabria, when I was informed that there was an urgent call from Palermo. I had learned to dread such moments, and I picked up the phone with my heart racing.

"The *carabinieri* arrested Totò Riina this morning!"

"What? Where?"

In amazement, I remembered the words I had said to a group of friends from Corleone who had come to visit me only a couple of weeks before. As always, the conversation at a certain point had turned to Totò Riina, the butcher who masterminded the Second

Mafia War. And I had said, "Totò Riina...! Totò Riina! You're still talking of Totò Riina...! A fortnight and he'll be arrested.... Can't you see that he's finished? Too many killings... He's been used even by politics but now he's finished."

I had meant it as a sardonic joke, but now it was true. After being on the run for twenty-three years, Totò Riina had at last been apprehended. He had been in his car with his driver on a routine errand. He was in Palermo—in his habitat. For a boss to be boss, he *must* remain in his territory and all his men must be aware that he is there, even if only very few trusted lieutenants know his precise whereabouts. During his bloody rise to power, Riina had stayed entrenched in his territory, between Corleone and Palermo. In those twenty-three years he had married a Corleone schoolteacher (in fact, three priests had officiated at the ceremony!) and had three children who were born in a private clinic in central Palermo, their births regularly registered and their baptisms sanctified. Now he was forced by the *carabinieri* to pose beneath a picture of General Carlo Alberto Dalla Chiesa, one of his most illustrious victims. Riina's photograph—that of a short, stocky, uncouth man with porcine eyes buried in the folds of an unprepossessing face—appeared on front pages and in television bulletins the world over.

People looked at this picture and asked themselves how we could have allowed such a man as this to become our ruler. They also wondered why Riina had been taken at this time, a moment that seemed to mark his highest achievement. The answer was that with the heat turned up as never before, he had been given up by a faction within Cosa Nostra who were anxious to placate law enforcement and give the impression that the Mafia had been decapitated.

| | |

A few weeks later, on May 9, 1993, beneath the well-preserved ancient Greek Temple of Concordia in Agrigento, a huge cross had been erected for Pope John Paul II's outdoor Mass. A year had elapsed since Falcone's death, a year marked by important arrests of wanted Commission members of Cosa Nostra, culminating in the apprehension of Riina. It was almost as if the state had awakened and decided, as it had in 1986 with the Maxitrial, to demonstrate that it was not merely an impotent bystander.

Sicilians were waiting to hear the Holy Father's words, wondering if the head of the Church would disappoint them again, as he had on that first visit in 1982. I was perturbed, also, and not only because of that previous event. Recently it had become clear that Bishop Cassisa of Monreale had been implicated with the Mafia in the misuse of construction funds. When I arrived at the airport to greet the Pope along with other officials, Cassisa was already in the receiving line. Noticing him, I turned around and left, aware that it was a significant breach of protocol. I saw the Holy Father several times later in the day and the subject didn't come up, but it seemed that he looked at me quizzically.

Pope John Paul II did not disappoint us this time. He repeatedly invoked the towering columns of the Temple of Concordia and its 2,500-year history, using it as a metaphor. "One of the temples is called 'of Concord,'" he said. "May its name be prophetic. May there be harmony in this your land. Harmony without deaths, without assassinations, without fears, without threats, without victims.... After so much suffering, you have the right to live in peace. Those guilty of disturbing this peace, bear on their consciences many human victims. They must understand that they cannot kill innocent beings. God once said: 'Do not kill.' No man, no human association, no Mafia can change and trample this most holy right of God." And then, raising his voice, he cried out: "In the name of Christ... I appeal to those responsible: Mafiosi convert! One day the judgment of God will come!"

The Pope had words for the Church as well—that Church which bore so much historical and cultural responsibility for what had happened in our land: "The Sicilian Church is called, today as it was yesterday, to share the commitment, the efforts and risks of those who fight, even at the cost of personal injury, to build a future of progress, of justice and peace for this island."

Again and again the Holy Father's words were interrupted by ovations from the hundred thousand people listening to him. It was like a rite of liberation from a hundred years of ecclesiastic *omertà*. When the Pope described the Mafia as a "sinful structure," he meant that any Mafioso, even if he himself had not committed mortal sins, was in a state of mortal sin by the mere fact of being a member of this organization. What he said was the theological equivalent of the criminal law passed a decade earlier, holding that to be a member of the Mafia, whatever your role, was to be involved in a criminal conspiracy.

When the Pope left Sicily that day, I went to the airport once again. I looked around and noticed that this time Bishop Cassisa was not present. As I stood in the receiving line to shake the Holy Father's hand, he took mine warmly in both of his and said, "Thank you for everything you've done. *Everything!*" As he said this last word with emphasis he looked intently into my eyes. What he said was probably open to interpretation, but the Pope, as much as any religious or lay prophet, was a master of gestures. I came away feeling that he was referring not only to what I had done in Palermo for the past several years, but also what I had done at the airport that morning.

| | |

Two days after the Pope's speech, a car bomb exploded in Rome. It had been meant for Maurizio Costanzo, the journalist who had hosted me on his show, but was triggered a second too late and his car got around a corner before the detonation. Costanzo's fault had been that of speaking too much and too often about the Mafia.

This attack was a prelude to a summer of violence in which Cosa Nostra decided to bring its attack into the heart of the country, waging an all-out offensive against established authority. In July, there were three car bombs on the same night. One near a Milan art gallery claimed five innocent victims. Then in Rome a bomb exploded in front of a magnificent Romanesque church, San Giorgio in Velabro, blowing its beautiful centuries-old portico to smithereens. A few minutes before, another car bomb had exploded at St. John Lateran, Rome's cathedral. This was a special message for John Paul II. (The Pope is also bishop of Rome, and St. John Lateran is the bishop's church.) To make the message even clearer, the bomb was aimed not at the front of the church but at the rear, where the Pope has his offices.

Cosa Nostra was saying that the Church could not attack the Mafia at the source, as the Pope had done in Agrigento. In addition to the bombing at St. John Lateran, there was another event that drove the lesson home. It took place in the Mafia-ridden district of Brancaccio in Palermo, where a priest named Father Pino Puglisi had a parish. Don Pino was a slim, middle-aged man with a gentle comportment and a boundless care for the children and youth of that difficult area. He lived his priesthood as a message of love, and in a district like Brancaccio that meant teaching his parishioners that they must not allow themselves to become objects of dominion. He did this quietly yet tenaciously, involving himself in parish work such as helping in the rehabilitation of young people addicted to the drugs that the Mafia spread throughout the neighborhood. He had organized a group of young antimafia volunteers and his parish had become committed to the effort to keep youth off the streets.

There were threats and warnings—the church door had been burnt—and Father Puglisi promptly denounced these attempts at intimidation from the pulpit during his homilies. But he also did his duty as a citizen, reporting to the police the existence of a wholesale market for drugs in the basement of a building not far from his church. At ten o'clock that very same night, as he was putting the key into the lock on his front door, a single shot in the head left him sprawled in a swelling puddle of blood on the pavement. He died soon afterward.[*]

---

[*] A few years later his assassin, turned into a *pentito*, said that Father Puglisi's last words were: *Me l'aspettavo.* "I thought as much."

Today the Church has set in motion the proceedings for the beatification of Father Puglisi, a man of faith martyred by the Mafia. That creates a message no one can mistake: there is no margin for compromise between faith in God and a criminal conspiracy that would usurp the place of God in our lives.

| | |

At times the Mafia's offensive of summer 1993 seemed like an attempted coup d'état. The Italian security service received a threat from the organization that it was at the point of recruiting Croatian terrorists to come into the country. There were rumors that the Mafia intended to poison supermarket food and strew the beaches of the Adriatic with syringes filled with HIV-infected blood, as part of a concerted effort to create a climate of fear that would drive tourists away. Yet those of us who got up each morning and breathlessly opened the newspapers to see if the Republic was still standing soon began to wonder if what we were seeing and hearing was actually the lashing tail of a dying dragon.

It was also in 1993 that the Palermo Prosecutor's Office began a formal investigation into charging Giulio Andreotti—seven times prime minister and member of nineteen governments between 1948 and 1992—with criminal association with the Mafia.

12

In 1993, Italy's voting law was changed so that citizens could choose their mayor in direct elections rather than vote for parties that would make this choice for them behind closed doors. When this happened, I immediately resigned from Parliament and returned home to run again for the only post I had ever really wanted: mayor of Palermo.

This prospect was not what it had formerly been. By now, some of the accomplishments of the Palermo Spring had been institutionalized, becoming part of the city's DNA. A sworn member of Cosa Nostra would never again occupy the mayor's office in Palazzo delle Aquile, for instance, as Vito Ciancimino once had. Gone too were the days when a covert, unwritten relationship with the Mafia could help a politician who maintained a façade of independence climb the greasy pole of power. Most importantly, the myth that the Mafiosi were part of an "honorable society" superior to civil society had been destroyed forever. The Mafia could no longer pull strings on its puppets within the system, which itself had changed— in Sicily and in Italy generally. The end of the Cold War and the effects of the "Clean Hands" campaign had revealed the old party alignments for what they were, and the Socialists and Christian Democrats had disintegrated with surprising speed. For the first time since the end of the Second World War, there would be truly free elections in Sicily.

Cosa Nostra was finally *outside* government, yet it remained a threat to our civic life, and our bodily lives. Those "subtle minds" that Giovanni Falcone had speculated about would always try to find a crevice in the system and, when the opportunity presented itself, crawl back into politics—influencing and intimidating voters, attempting to suborn political figures. They would not hesitate to use violence to gain their ends, and so my problem would be staying alive until election day.

Early in the campaign, I went to see Antonino Caponnetto, Falcone's and Borsellino's old boss in the Antimafia Pool. He was running for city council as a member of La Rete, and his offices were in an apartment that I owned on Via Rosolino Pilo, just a few blocks away from my own campaign headquarters. I jumped into my car and began looking at some documents as the driver pulled off. After fifteen minutes, when we should have long since arrived at Caponnetto's office, I realized that we seemed to be going around in circles quite a distance from where we should have been.

"What's the matter?" I asked the bodyguard riding shotgun for the driver. "Have you forgotten where Via Rosolino Pilo is?"

"I'm sorry," the officer answered, "but we've been informed that a stolen car has been found in front of Doctor Caponnetto's offices. We're waiting for the explosives experts to arrive."

My reaction was irrational, but for some reason I saw red. My bodyguards were only doing their duty and they were perfectly right, but something in me suddenly snapped. If I let myself be intimidated now, my life would become a melodrama of fear.

"Look, this is the way the whole campaign is going to be, so we'd all better get used to it! Now take me to Via Rosolino Pilo immediately!"

Of course the officer argued—he was responsible for my safety—but I got angrier and angrier, and ended up calling the minister of the interior in Rome on my cell phone. By the time I got through, the explosives experts had determined that the car in question was clean, and I finally found myself in Caponnetto's offices. Looking at the faces of all the young volunteers in the rooms, people who were supporting me as well as Caponnetto and who expected that I would live long enough to make Palermo once and for all a city of light, I suddenly felt unsteady and had to sit down.

Apart from this moment of tension, two odd experiences from that campaign stick in my mind. One of them involved the son of an old Mafia boss who was openly saying that he was going to vote for me, without calling down any displeasure from his father. I was certainly not going to permit any Mafioso to jump onto my bandwagon. So I contacted the police and asked them if they had a way of finding out if there was something sinister behind this declaration. They had their undercover agents ask the young man's father directly what was happening. "If I try to prevent my son from voting for Orlando, he'll do it anyway," the boss said. "So either I lose as a man of honor, or I lose as a father. In this case, better the first than the second." This was exactly the dilemma I wanted such people to face: being forced to choose between family ties and Mafia ties.

The other episode unfolded one day as I was campaigning in a Mafia-infested part of Palermo called Cep, going from shop to shop and speaking to as many people as I could. At one point I walked into a butcher shop, where one of the people present watched nervously for a while and then said, "Sir, Don Giovanni wants to speak to you."

I looked around for somebody in a cassock. (In Italian, *Don* is often prefixed to a priest's name in sign of respect.) There was only a huge man sitting at a cash register, looking me up and down with an air of authority. I had no idea who he was or why he particularly wished to speak to me, but the nervousness of my escort told me that *they* knew who Don Giovanni was. When I walked up to him, the immense man glared at me and pointed his finger:

"Damn you!" he roared. "You've ruined me and my family with your fucking 'Mafia! Mafia! Mafia!'... Two of my brothers are in the clink, my son's on the run.... Thanks to your fucking 'Mafia' we've been tried and condemned... damn you!"

My escort had their hands on their guns. They had sandwiched me so tightly between their bodies that I could hardly breathe. I was transfixed by the large man's inflamed face. He surprised us all with what he said next.

Ma sapi chi ci ricu? Lei avi un paru ri cugghiuna! "But you know what? You got balls!" It was a clear profession of hatred, and also an open admission of defeat.

When the polls closed on election day, I was in my campaign headquarters on Via Villafranca, in the building where I was born. Those austere rooms from my cloistered youth were full of excited young activists answering phones, taking down results as they began pouring in, preparing the champagne for the victory celebration that the exit polls had already assured us. In spite of intermittent rain, the street outside was full of people—so full that traffic had been stopped and detoured. As the first returns were announced over the radio, we looked out the windows at impromptu dances beginning in the streets and people laughing and embracing. I had intended to wait for the final results, but I decided to step out onto the small balcony overlooking the street and say a few words.

Palermo è nostra! someone yelled before I could get started. *E non di Cosa Nostra!* echoed another voice, punning on the word *nostra.*

Before I could say anything, the crowd took up the chant: *Palermo… è nostra… e non di Cosa Nostra!* "Palermo is ours… and not the Cosa Nostra's!"

When the final results were in, I won with 75.2 percent of the vote, a majority unequalled by the mayor of any other Italian city that year. In the next few unforgettable hours, soaked to the skin by the drizzling rain and surrounded by joyous faces in the Piazza Pretoria, which had seen so many outpourings of grief, I felt that we might yet make it.

Fifteen days later there was another round of celebrations when Corleone, at the second ballot—no candidate got a majority on the first one—also elected a young mayor committed to reform. Democracy had come to the belly of the beast. Hundreds of young people sang and shouted in the streets of that town, once a worldwide symbol of the Mafia, now proudly a new symbol of the antimafia. They danced through the streets, deliberately detouring to pass under the windows of the modest two-storied house where Totò Riina had lived with his wife and children. Never before had anyone dared so much.

Always before, Sicily had been caught in a pendular history—long periods of equilibrium broken by episodes of violence, followed by a new commitment on the part of the government to control the Mafia, which always eventually failed. But something had changed with the deaths of Falcone and Borsellino. This time it seemed possible that the Mafia pendulum would not swing back again.

| | |

Palermo had its spring at the end of the eighties—a season of slogans, messages, hopes and the first tender buds of freedom. Now in the nineties, it had its summertime—a renaissance of achievements and a flowering of democracy.

I had large ambitions for my new administration, but we began with small measures that would make government work on a daily basis. I had tried to do this during my first term as mayor, but at that time, Cosa Nostra was still inside the state, and as a result, municipal personnel, many owing their jobs to the Mafia, subverted our efforts. Now, we put rules in place to ensure that all employees owed their jobs to their qualifications, and our citizens began to give the idea of government another chance.

We concentrated on equipping the municipality and all its offices with a centralized computer system. I realize that claiming this as an achievement in the last decade of the twentieth century will seem almost ridiculous to anybody accustomed to living in a normal modern city, but in the early nineties Palermo was still not a normal city. Simply getting a minor building permit or a birth or death certificate or a tax form from the city clerk's office was a frustrating, time-consuming business, and over the years a shadowy figure, the *spicciafacienni* or "business expeditor," had become a fixture in our municipal life. Such individuals lounged outside the Palermo Registry Office, waiting to be paid to go from office to office or from counter to counter in a citizen's place, transacting his or her business and eventually producing the desired document. Of course, the *spicciafacienni* made his way by passing out small bribes to the clerks behind the counter, and he got what he needed while citizens who couldn't afford his services waited interminably in line.

We did away with all that. Official documents and information can now simply be obtained from automated machines, similar to ATMs. The transaction is swift, with no margin for corruption. The requested document comes directly to the citizen, without the intervention of a middleman. It may seem like merely another bureaucratic procedure to people who live in places where the bureaucracy works, but in Palermo it was a gift of autonomy.

| | |

We understood that creating a renaissance in a city trying to free itself from the dead hand of totalitarianism was like waging a war, and that victory would come about only as the result of an integrated, all-out campaign. So we decided to move on four inter-related fronts at once: the media, the culture, the schools, and the physical condition of the city—all for one objective, the creation of a civic consciousness based on the rule of law.

The media were in many ways our most subtle but also our most profound difficulty. As I have already indicated, the conspiracy of silence about the Mafia and its assault on Sicilian life was so successful that it created a sort of parallel universe. While we were being subverted by illegality and murder, the newspapers and television stations created the picture of a "normal" society, with perhaps a little more crime than other European societies, but otherwise not remarkably different. The key to this fantasy was the media's refusal for decades to say the word "Mafia," and then in the late 1970s, when it was impossible to keep from saying it any longer, to cover the phenomenon as if it were a local problem involving gangsters killing each other.

This was a weakness in the national press, and even more in the Sicilian press. Our regional newspapers were torn between the mandate to provide truthful reporting and the fear that by doing so they would worsen Sicily's image. Most of our citizens knew what was happening, but until as late as the 1980s, everyone agreed it was best to keep silent and not denounce the Mafia. As I became familiar with the dilemmas of our city, I saw that we would never be rid of Mafia domination until we had a free and aggressive press.

I was particularly disturbed by the editorial line on this issue taken by our newspaper of record, the *Giornale di Sicilia*. During the years of the Second Mafia War, the *Giornale* professed a sort of agnosticism about the problems posed by the Mafia. After the Dalla Chiesa assassination, when it was no longer possible for anyone to remain mute, the paper started talking about the Mafia, but its reporting was now too punctilious, too careful not to deviate—as the editors put it—from "impartiality." In practice this meant, for instance, that the paper conscientiously reported the words of those who accused the Antimafia Pool of Prosecutors of abusing their prerogatives and forming a cult of personality. And it printed sensationalized news accounts, under banner headlines, of the tragic accident in which Paolo Borsellino's escort accidentally struck a group of schoolchildren at a bus stop.

The impact of the *Giornale*'s reporting on the Mafia was magnified by the fact that Palermo was a one-newspaper city. I couldn't find a way out of the difficulty this posed for our efforts at reform. Finally in 1989 I simply decided that I would no longer talk to anyone from the *Giornale di Sicilia*. The editors demanded to know why. I told them that normal European cities have more than one paper, and I would not talk again to a reporter from the *Giornale* until another daily was sold on the streets of Palermo.

It seemed a little quixotic—even to me—at the time. But by 1993, when I was campaigning for mayor, this decision had begun to have an impact. These elections were the most important event in Palermo, and the paper of record was not getting the inside story. (It was like Giuliani not speaking to the *New York Times,* one local newsman told me accusatorily.) Not only did I not give the *Giornale* interviews, I ordered my assistants to keep its reporters a hundred feet away from me at all times. I also refused to talk to representatives of the paper's television station, the most important one in Palermo.

I was trying to make a point about journalistic ethics. But I was also, like Cosa Nostra itself, trying to send a message. Mine was a constructive message: that civil society could not remain uncommitted on the issue of the Mafia any longer.

On the night of my landslide victory, no reporter from the *Giornale* was granted an interview, although I spoke with every other Italian and foreign newspaper and television station covering the elections. From that day onward, the paper began to exhibit a different, more responsible approach to news about the city administration and the antimafia movement. Six months later, a second newspaper, *Il Mediterraneo,* opened in Palermo. On the day of its first edition, I spoke to a reporter from *Giornale di Sicilia* for the first time in four years.

In a remarkable turnaround, the *Giornale* soon became a strong supporter of reform and civic openness. This support was particularly important in the efforts we were making to implant a culture of freedom in the schools. The paper's editors and I came to an agreement: they would print a daily page called "class assignment," featuring articles by kids about their schools and neighborhoods—why there were double sessions, broken windows, no supplies, and so on. And I would write by hand a note to each of the children whose letter had been published the previous day, answering his or her questions and whenever possible promising to solve the problem. Then, a policeman would hand-deliver this note to the student at school. The editors of the *Giornale* agreed with me that we accomplished many things at once by doing this: we showed that a free press serves the citizenry, that speaking out gets results, and that the police are part of this process.

| | |

As Palermo slowly—and miraculously, for those of us who watched it happen—became a city with a free and enquiring media, we also tried to move ahead in our effort to renew the culture as it was experienced every day by our citizens. It was a daunting job, whose challenge was symbolized for me by our effort to disinter our grand, early-sixteenth-century Gothic church called Santa Maria dello Spasimo.

Through the centuries the Spasimo had been used not only as a church, but also as a theater, a warehouse, a leper colony, a hospital, and an old people's home. It had been badly damaged by bombing in World War II, and then what remained of it, abandoned and crumbling, was used as a dump for construction materials during the Mafia's Sack of Palermo. It had since become piles of rubble where intrepid urchins played by day and junkies would sneak in at night for a fix. People had forgotten the role it had once played in our civic life.

During my first term as mayor in the mid-eighties, I decided that restoring this former gem would be a good place to begin in our effort to reclaim our city. I had sent in trucks to remove tons of debris. The Spasimo had been cleaned and prepared for an inaugural piano concert. On the day before the event, the stage, sitting beneath a soaring Gothic arch, had been burnt by Mafiosi who thus made it clear that they regarded this part of the city as belonging to them and not to the people. My friend Enzo Bianco, at that time mayor of Catania, the second largest city in Sicily, immediately came to the rescue with a mobile stage, so we had a concert in spite of the fire. Paolo Borsellino sat in the audience, visibly moved by hearing music in a beautiful historic setting only a few blocks away from where he had grown up.

Then the following day, part of a wall collapsed and the Spasimo once more had to be shut down. And so it remained throughout the time I was out of office as mayor.

Now, after I had been returned to office, this time as a result of direct elections, we decided to take up the project again. In the meantime our administration had encouraged former prisoners coming out of Ucciardone prison to form cooperatives to make a livelihood, rather than returning to their Mafia lives. Interestingly, the low bidder on the contract for the Spasimo's cleanup was a cooperative of ex-convicts headed by a man named Filippo Abbate. Within a few months he and his workers had restored the remaining walls of the church and what had once been the attached hospital, creating a garden that included fully grown trees, sculptured paths and benches. On the day of the area's dedication in July 1995, police officials and *carabinieri* mixed with Abbate and his ex-cons. "When I go back home in the evening and I look my children in the face," Abbate told me a few days later, "I'm no longer ashamed of myself."

There was a sad epilogue to this story. A short time after the completion of the work on the Spasimo, Filippo Abbate, his wife and two children died in a car crash on mainland Italy where they were on holiday. When I was informed of this tragic accident, I went to the Abbate home in the Kalsa to express my condolences to his remaining family. As I embraced his grieving mother, she said to me: "My son adored you. You convinced him that he had to work...." And then his sister-in-law murmured: "Filippo's brothers, Gino and Giovanni, should be allowed to be present at the funeral."

The problem was that Gino (a Mafioso known as *Gino mitra*, or "Machine-gun Gino") was an inmate of Ucciardone and Giovanni was in another prison. I went to see the chief of police and explained the situation, insisting on the importance of being able to show Filippo's family and neighbors and the residents of the Kalsa that the government was demanding but also capable of humanity. Two days later, when Filippo Abbate's coffin was carried from his home to the Spasimo for the funeral ceremony, I shouldered it part of the way. Machine-gun Gino and Giovanni had been allowed to bid their brother a last farewell in person the day before. (A couple of months later, the magistrate who supervised Ucciardone told me that after Filippo's funeral, the behavior of Gino and the other Mafia inmates improved. He told me: "They say, *U Sinnacu Orlando è un gran curmutu cu 'sta camurria di antimafia, ma havi cori.* Mayor Orlando is a big cuckold with this antimafia crap, but he has a heart.")

Restoring the Spasimo was like throwing a stone in the city planning reservoir, causing waves to lap on other shores. Because of the hundreds of visitors that the Spasimo and its cultural events attracted, the surrounding area completely changed. Bars and small trattorias sprang up, and souvenir shops opened. Those doing business there would ensure that the area was kept clean and file a report if a streetlight was not working.

The Spasimo functioned as our research and development project. After we cleaned it up, we turned to another area which had been closed for decades and allowed to deteriorate. This was around a twelfth-century Arab-Norman castle, the Zisa Castle. (In fact, when a Palermitan wants to indicate a countless number of problems or obstacles in the way of completing some project, he often says, "As many as the devils of the Zisa," because the ceiling in one of the castle's halls is frescoed with innumerable fantastic demons, and tradition says that nobody has ever been able to count exactly how many there are.)

One day our commissioner for culture and I went to visit what had once been an enormous furniture factory, built at the end of the 1800s right next to the Zisa Castle. Covering almost 200,000 square feet, it had been used during World War I as assembly sheds for fighter-bombers for the Italian, English and French governments, before returning to its original function of producing world-famed art nouveau chairs. The factory had then been abandoned and its sheds rapidly fell into decay. This vestige of nineteenth century industrial architecture was supposed to have been ripped down to make way for "residential construction" during the Mafia's Sack of Palermo in the 1950s. But Italy's notorious administrative inefficiency helped save the day, and the former assembly rooms of the factory were still standing. My culture commissioner and I had the same idea at the same time: here was an enormous space that could become a cultural center—*I Cantieri Culturali alla Zisa.*

Rather than wait for funding to take on the whole project at once, we began to restore the rooms one by one. The first of these, the Galleria Bianca or White Gallery, was soon opened for art exhibitions, followed by a second for theatrical productions, then a third for a theater school and a fourth for music rehearsals. Then we had the idea that because Sicily is such a melting pot of different cultures, religions and ideas, we would offer an area where students could contemplate this diversity. The Library of Difference, as we decided to call it, contains a reading room where citizens can consult books about Sicily's past, and hold meetings and debates on the idea of cultural differences—what binds us and what can also tear us apart.

We wanted the Zisa Cultural Center to attract whole families, not just intellectuals. So we designed gardens and a playground for children, along with a cafeteria. Soon *I Cantieri Culturali* was a top attraction for Palermitans and tourists too. Because of the area's size, it was an evolving development. Today work proceeds on the most ambitious project in the center, a contemporary art museum which will have a world-class art collection and also offer artists work spaces to create the classics of the future.

| | |

The great symbol of our movement for civic renewal, however, was the Teatro Massimo. Designed by Palermo's great architect Filippo Basile, the opera house was seventy-seven years old when it was closed "temporally" for "urgent work" in 1974. The contract for rehabilitation, worth several million dollars, was immediately awarded to a company with Mafia connections. Not surprisingly, the years passed, the money disappeared, and the Teatro Massimo fell further into disuse. During two decades of decline, it was partly reopened only once—fittingly, to allow the filming of the opera scenes in *The Godfather Part III* and the concluding sequence when

Al Pacino's daughter is killed at the top of the imposing flight of steps leading up to the entrance. Palermo's opera lovers meanwhile were constantly assured that it would only be a matter of months before the Massimo reopened. But the only part of it used during those years was the former Press Club in one of its basement rooms, where men like Vito Ciancimino and Stefano Bontate played cards with their cronies.

Precisely because it had become such a stark symbol of the forces robbing our city of its vitality and control over its own civic destiny, I had tried to do something about the Teatro Massimo in my first years as mayor during the eighties. The municipal, regional and national powers all refused to help. In the nineties, though, the situation was more favorable and I found that another round of funds might be available, especially if there were guarantees that they would not also vanish unaccounted. Some complained: Why, with the multitude of problems that faced us, should an opera house be a top priority? For me the answer was easy. I knew that reopening the Teatro Massimo would be the most tangible signal that Palermo was indeed undergoing a renaissance, just as in 1946 the first sign of rebirth in war-ravaged Milan had been the reconstruction of La Scala.

I began a legal battle which would enable the city to regain total control of the building. Once that happened, the restoration began again. Just as with the Zisa Cultural Center, we thought it important not to wait for the total renovation to be completed before opening the theater to the people. We believed that if citizens could see the work taking place, they would set aside their natural cynicism about politicians' promises.

When it came time to plan the opening event, we looked for a prestigious international orchestra to perform alongside the Teatro's own. We settled on the great Berlin Philharmonic, whose director, Claudio Abbado, is not only Italian himself, but the son of a Palermitan mother. Moreover, his reputation as an exacting critic of his orchestra's venues is such that the people would realize that if he brought his orchestra to the Massimo, it meant that we had done our work well. Late in 1995, I went to Berlin to meet Maestro Abbado in a Sicilian restaurant in downtown Berlin. At the end of the meeting, Abbado agreed in principle to direct the Massimo's opening concert, but only if the theater was really in top condition and only if a definite date had been set for the later, full opening for opera—what the Massimo had been made for. He knew enough about Palermo to refuse to participate in a limited reopening for political purposes.

We settled on an opening night in May 1997, which would mark the hundredth anniversary of the Massimo's construction. That gave us less than a year and a half in which to complete what had not been accomplished in over twenty years. In a race against time, we reached out to private sponsors. I was pleased that the *Giornale di Sicilia* stepped up immediately, not only agreeing to make a donation that would underwrite the restoration of the entire Gallery, but also publicizing in its pages what it called "Operation Massimo," printing each day a countdown showing how much money was still required to complete the project. This brought forth entrepreneurs who donated money and artisans who donated talent.

Work proceeded around the clock, day and night. May 12, 1997, was to be opening night; the renovation was finished at 8:45 that morning.

The Berlin Philharmonic had arrived in town the previous day. At 9:00 A.M. on May 12, the orchestra's acoustics expert was ushered in. Solemnly he took his place on the director's podium, looked around, lifted his right hand and struck his tuning fork. A single, pure note rang and died away.

"*Nein.*"

The German negative seemed to sound the death knell for the Massimo, and for the credibility of my administration. The workers looked at each other, their exhausted, bloodshot eyes filled with despair.

Mesmerized, everybody watched this man who held our fate in his hands as he looked around searchingly. "Perhaps... it could be this drape you've put around the podium," he said in German. The beautiful velvet covering was quickly ripped away and the wood-workers began repairing the spot.

At four o'clock that afternoon, two hours before the theater was officially due to open, the tuning fork sounded again and this time came the magic word.

"*Ja!*"

For weeks, in the markets and at the bars in Palermo's outdoor sitting areas on the streets, conversation had centered on whether the Massimo would be finished in time. People who had never attended an opera or symphony in their lives were treating this as if it were the World Cup. Who would win, the forces of action or the forces of inertia? When it became clear that we would make our deadline, the *Giornale di Sicilia's* local TV station decided to broadcast the concert live, both on their channel and on two giant outdoor screens for the people who would not be able to get in: one in Piazza Pretoria and another in Piazza Verdi, the square beside the Massimo itself.

In spite of a threat of rain, by mid-afternoon both piazzas were packed. When the audience began arriving and mounting the stairs toward the entrance under the mighty columns, Palermo's citizens applauded, almost as if each single person entering the Massimo should be cheered as a testimonial to this great victory.

I entered the theater—running late, as usual, but still in time for an emotional moment. Before beginning his Brahms program, Abbado lifted his baton and we heard the yearning notes and words of Verdi's chorus from *Nabucco*, sung by the Massimo's own choir with its orchestra: *Va pensiero sull'ali dorate*... "Fly memory on golden wings..." This was the last music heard at the Massimo twenty-three years before, in the final performance before it closed. Now, on those same notes, it was returning to life. Once the sounds of Verdi had faded, the Berlin Philharmonic Orchestra went on to play the First and Third symphonies of Johannes Brahms.

Afterward, following interminable curtain calls, we all went down the Massimo's steps—no longer the steps on which the scene of a Mafia murder had been filmed, but once again steps leading to a great opera theater. The square was full of cheering people, and the going forth of all those who had pulled off this miracle seemed to anticipate the triumphal march from *Aida*, which in fact opened the Massimo's opera season a few months later.

| | |

The Spasimo, the Zisa, and the Massimo were the jewels, but the crown itself comprised the 158 churches, 400 palazzi, 55 monasteries and 7 theaters that needed to be saved from the status of "abomination" to which the Mafiosi and their sympathizers had condemned them in order to tear them down. After the years of neglect and decay, the challenge that faced us was enormous, yet we were committed to bringing these structures back to their old splendor.

We restored and cleaned, paved roads and fixed sewers. Old fountains, for so many years dry and neglected, once more spouted water, and where the space permitted, we created green areas. People directly affected, especially residents and shopkeepers, were invited to assemblies and meetings where the plans were discussed, and their suggestions and needs—perhaps not imagined by the planners—were considered and possibly incorporated in the project.

It took large sums to restore these buildings properly, ensuring safety yet respecting the original structures. But the money was found, provided in part by the European Community, in part by the Sicilian Region, and in part by the municipality itself. And to encourage private owners to restore their own properties—many of them had simply abandoned their houses during the years Palermo was under the gun—we made financial grants of up to 40 percent of the costs of rehabilitation on the condition that the owner get his plans approved by the city. These grants produced an extraordinary result: the population of the historical center, which had been dwindling through the years, began to grow. The heart of the old city began to beat once more.

At the same time that the city was shedding its sullen look, the

Department of Education was picking up our unfinished business from the 1980s. Back then, in certain districts as much as 40 percent of the children either didn't complete school or didn't attend at all. The result was a level of illiteracy or semiliteracy unacceptable for any normal, modern city. We took that as a challenge. By the late 1990s, this dropout rate decreased by two-thirds, and—miraculously, for anyone who knew what schooling had been in our city a few years earlier—the Italian Institute for Statistics cited Palermo schools as an example for the rest of the country.

We wanted to educate children in basic intellectual and academic skills. We also wanted to educate them to protect their heritage and thus keep it from ever being stolen again by Cosa Nostra. This is how Palermo's "Adopt a Monument" program arose. The inaugural ceremony was held in February 1995 in Palermo's magnificent art nouveau theater, Teatro Politeama. Because we recognized the role of memory in recovering our history, the project was dedicated to the memory of Giovanni Falcone, Francesca Morvillo, Paolo Borsellino "and all those who had given their lives for the freedom of Palermo."

There I was on the stage, wearing my official mayor's sash—green, white and red, the colours of the Italian flag, bordered with gold tassels—and flanked by two municipal employees in high uniform, by Maria Falcone and Rita Borsellino, sisters of the martyred magistrates, and by other family members of Mafia victims. Looking out at the sea of excited children's faces, I said, "Just as an adopted child is a child who was abandoned but will be loved and cared for by its new parents, so you will be the parents of the monument you are adopting. You will have to learn to know it and love it, learn to look after it and teach others to love and respect it. Remember, the more it has been neglected, the more love will it need."

The children of each school or class participating in the program had elected a representative who then came up onto the stage. Rita Borsellino and Maria Falcone handed each representative an official "adoption certificate" I had signed. Then every child present was given a medal especially designed for the occasion with Palermo's emblem on it, an eagle with half-spread wings.

Never in our wildest dreams had we imagined that the project would meet with such great success. So intense was the children's participation, that their enthusiasm soon infected their teachers, families and neighbors. With the help of their teachers, the children first carried out in-depth investigation into the history of "their" monument, not only doing book research, but also interviewing local experts and—even more important—elderly inhabitants whose reawakened memories yielded uncollected data about the past, and who as a consequence were made to feel that what they recalled would restore some coherence to Palermo's damaged history.

Thanks to the enthusiasm and tenacity of these young adoptive "parents," individuals also began to sponsor the restoration of their local monument, vying with each other as to whose monument would be reopened first. Previously, there had not been much of a tradition of community work in Palermo. But now entrepreneurs, members of Lion's or Rotary Clubs, or simply the butcher around the corner, came forward with funds and began to lobby for this or that monument to be restored.

In the United States this would be a heartwarming little story about community spirit. It was that for Palermo, but it was also something more profound: a story of people long denied a map to their lives now regaining control of their own territory, reclaiming it from enemy hands. Palermo used to be like a desert full of tents, each belonging to a different family, clan, confraternity, social class or political group, with the area between a no-man's land that belonged to no one and nobody cared about. The Adopt a Monument program changed all this. It planted the seeds of awareness about the *res publica*, the "public thing" that belongs to everyone— an awareness that what is not "yours" or "mine" is *ours* and must be jointly cared for. As soon as the citizens begin to take control of public space, the *capomafia* knows that his time is past.

When the program began, over 80 percent of Palermo's great

architectural moments were permanently closed. Within a few years, 160 monuments were adopted, with over 60 percent of them open once again and the rest being restored. The Department of Education has published several volumes containing the extraordinary historical research, drawings and interviews about these civic monuments done by the students. Can youngsters who have put so much effort, energy, love and pride into discovering and bringing back their heritage allow an outside force to come in once again and steal it from them? I don't think so. I believe they will continue to love and protect not only their "own" monument, but all the others in the city as well. I also believe that a city whose public spaces are loved and protected is a city where the margins for illegality are narrow.

| | |

Another step in reviving our city, which had been so needy, was to recognize the needs of others. At the same time that our renaissance was going forward, the international press was full of stories about the atrocities of civil war in the region of Abkhazia, part of the young, independent republic of Georgia. We all saw harrowing pictures of desperate families fleeing their homes and flooding into Tbilisi, the capital and also Palermo's sister city, which had offered me, my wife and daughters sanctuary at a time when the Italian state could not guarantee my security. I had a personal moral debt to Georgia, and I could not forget the letter that Eduard Shevardnadze, the Georgian president, had sent me when he was still Mikhail Gorbachev's foreign minister, expressing both his personal solidarity and that of his country in "the battle for Palermo."

In 1994 I contacted the authorities in Tbilisi and offered to host three hundred Georgian children from the Abkhazia region who would come to Palermo for three or four months in the summer. I welcomed the children, all of them orphans, at the airport that first summer—pale, frightened faces with huge eyes, and thin bodies. I watched the host families embrace their children and saw the determined gleam in many a Sicilian mamma's eye—women determined to fatten up these poor little souls, to cuddle and spoil, to bring color and smiles to those drawn faces. It was the innate generosity typical of the Sicilian people, but there was also an understanding on the part of people who themselves had been victims of domination.

After that first year, an association of families sprang up to perpetuate this program. Now, the four hundred or so Georgian children who arrive each year are cared for on private initiative, by people who are so confident they have come into their own, that they have something left over to give others. Last year I received a fax from Mr. Shevardnadze's office which thanked us and said proudly, "This year we are in a condition to pay for the fuel for the children's Tbilisi-Palermo flight. Unfortunately as yet we cannot also pay for their return flight, but as of next year we believe that the Georgian government will be able to cover the entire cost."

| | |

In 1994 I decided run for the European Parliament. I knew it would mean exhausting travels to and from Brussels and Strasbourg where the parliament sits, extra work and extra energy, particularly if I continued to do justice to my job as mayor. But I also knew that, although it had been beaten back in Sicily, the Mafia was on the rise as an international phenomenon and thus the fight against it had to become equally international. This was something that law enforcement bodies had known for years, but the legislatures of many European countries did not sufficiently acknowledge. Actually, I should say Mafias in the plural, since the phenomenon of organized crime had grown tenfold since the disintegration of the Soviet Union and its satellite states. An international Mafia had penetrated Europe financially and criminally. Now it was necessary to build a European antimafia as well.

A Euro MP generally considers himself successful if he gets one piece of legislation passed during his tenure. Because of the admitted importance of the organized crime issue, I got three bills passed, all dealing with problems posed by Mafia criminality. The first, which I asked to be called the Falcone Program in honor of my murdered friend, mandated the exchange of information, data, know-how and resources between law enforcement, intelligence, investigative bodies and the judiciary of the various European Union countries. The point I made in arguing for this law was that if Giovanni Falcone and Rudolph Giuliani had not shared information and know-how, the whole Pizza Connection drug trafficking network linking Sicily and the United States would never have been dismantled. There can be no boundaries to the fight against the Mafia.

My second resolution urged that Italian law holding simple *membership* in a Mafia association to be a criminal offense be extended to all EU member countries. There are some in Italy, of course, who have argued that such a law is a violation of civil liberties—an argument that was also advanced in the debates before the European Parliament. My response was simply that Cosa Nostra and other Mafia-type organizations—the Chinese Triads, the Russian Mafia and the Colombian cartels, to mention only three—are not exactly debating societies one joins to promote ideas. They are criminal organizations trafficking in arms, drugs, nuclear material, human beings and anything else that will turn a profit.

The third resolution passed by the European Parliament was also based on an Italian law, the Rognoni–La Torre Law, which establishes the right of the state to seize assets that are the fruit of Mafia criminal activity. In arguing for this resolution, I pointed out that such a law hits Mafiosi where it hurts most: in the wallet. Unless this law is applied in other countries as well as in Italy, the Mafia will simply invest elsewhere—as in fact it has been doing for years. Many British citizens would be horrified to discover how many of their hotels, restaurants, even country estates are owned by Mafia families. And the same goes for many citizens of Vienna who would be flabbergasted if they knew how many of the elegant hotels in their beautiful capital are Mafia-owned. And all those sun worshippers on the beaches of the fabled Costa del Sol in Spain might sleep a little less easily if they knew that many of the wonderful resorts there were developed with Mafia money.

For decades, Sicily had been exporting an extremely dangerous disease. Now for the first time, through this European legislation, we were exporting a new and strong medicine to combat that disease. All those years, we had been part of the problem, but now we became part of the solution.

13

"**L**uchetto, be careful or you'll die!"

That old warning from my doting parents had become a sort of curse in my youth when I was struggling to find a place for myself outside the confining aristocratic identity into which I had been born. But it was also a warning that I should have heeded more in the past few years. In our war against the Mafia, I had been pushing myself too hard, averaging three or four hours of sleep a night for weeks on end and drinking countless cups of espresso every day to keep going. Although I was always on the move, it was in and out of planes and armored cars, activity that never provided any real physical exercise. I ate haphazardly and always unhealthily, and had put on a lot of weight.

Late in 1994, I came down with one bout of bronchitis after another. I ignored it, going about my work as usual and as a result winding up in the hospital with pneumonia. I wasn't particularly bothered, remembering the first time I was in the hospital for this disease as a boy, when I had discovered Stendhal. Then, after a couple of days, the chief physician came into my room with a disturbed look on his face. "I'm afraid it's not just pneumonia," he said. "You have lung cancer."

It was a strange moment. Once the idea of cancer had time to penetrate my mind, the first thing I felt was relief. It was almost as if an unbearable weight had been lifted from me. Thinking about it later, I realized that the conviction that I was going to die a violent death had become so much a part of me that the prospect of dying like anybody else, of "natural" causes, made me suddenly feel like a normal human being.

Because Palermo's renaissance was still in a tentative phase, I didn't want news of my illness to be made public. And I knew that if I remained in the hospital too long, in a city so accustomed to whispering, talk about my health would soon begin and inevitably be used by politicians still tied to the Mafia and looking for a political comeback. So after a few days in the hospital I came home, returning every few days for a "normal" checkup.

Perhaps the worst moment was one Saturday afternoon when, as I lay in bed at home, the telephone rang. It was the most esteemed lung specialist in Sicily and he spoke bluntly: "Look, Luca, I know I'm not your personal physician, but I've seen your x-rays and your CAT scan and there's absolutely no time to be wasted. I've already fixed you an appointment for tomorrow in a clinic in Milan where they will operate immediately. If you act now, you still might make it. But it's possible that your days are numbered."

I put down the phone. So this was the end of the road. But at least I would die in my bed and not in the streets of Palermo, another of those illustrious corpses floating in a pool of blood on the pavement.

My family doctor was less certain that I should act immediately. I could tell that he didn't want me to rush into radical treatment. I agreed with him that I would wait and see what developed. Only later did I discover that he had secretly flown to Milan after my examinations with all my x-rays and exam data, and consulted with Italy's most respected medical experts.

The weeks went by. The shadowy area in my lungs continued to show up in x-rays, but didn't seem to be growing larger. Doctors punctured my chest with long needles to do biopsies, which also yielded ambiguous results. But then, as time passed, new x-rays showed that the shadow was shrinking. This continued over a period of several months until it disappeared entirely. What I had had was a very serious case of pneumonia with complications of the pleura. Now I was born again and had a leftover life to live.

| | |

For the first time since I had committed myself to politics, I spent long stretches of time with my family. And as far as my girls were concerned, that meant for the first time since they were born. They surrounded me with affection and care, and slowly I began discovering how precious were these relationships that I had so long taken for granted. I had given everything to my public life and little or nothing to my private life.

My convalescence at home in Palermo was rewarding and enriching, but I still felt tension from my bout of near-cancer. In addition, the electoral victory of Silvio Berlusconi's Liberty Alliance weighed heavily on me. It seemed to block any real change in the country and in Sicily, even though the Berlusconi government fell after only seven months. Finally I decided to try to put all this behind me. Milli and I planned to go for two weeks to a health clinic in Bressanone in the northeast of the country, in the Italian region of Alto Adige near the Austrian border. I would dedicate fifteen days to recovery.

The clinic was a large building in typical Sud-Tirol style on the bank of Bressanone's river Adige, surrounded by a beautifully tended park. It was spring, the mountain air had a mentholated smell, and the sun sparkled on the lush green of perfect lawns. This was going to be paradise.

We were welcomed by Frau Maria, the soft-spoken governess, exuding efficiency and discipline that called up memories of my childhood's Fräulein. We were shown to our rooms and informed that the treatment would start immediately—with a water diet to cleanse the impurities from the system. Water and only water. Milli and I exchanged apprehensive looks. Outside on the lawn, deck chairs beckoned from beside garden tables, on each of which sat glasses and a jug of water—only water. When I went to bed that night, the rumblings of my stomach disturbed the silence.

The day began very early, at 6 A.M., when I was awakened by a Wagnerian Siegfried—tall, blond, blue-eyed, broad-shouldered— who stalked into the room, yanked off the bedclothes, accompanied me to an immaculate white basement, laid me on a sort of table and began pounding on my body. After this brutal massage, he disappeared. I was just beginning to revive when he suddenly returned, carrying a large sack of heated grain, which he dumped on my stomach. I yelled. As I lay there beaten and burned, Siegfried asked, "You already feel better, don't you?"

I nodded in hopes of not provoking him further, but then the masseur nodded toward the shower and ordered, "In there!"

I felt relieved by the thought of recuperating in warm water, tilting my face up to receive it and allowing it to wash gently over my aching body. But I yelled out and gasped for breath when Siegfried turned on a frozen jet. Hastily I emerged and groped for my gown.

"*Gut, ja?*" smiled Siegfried. "Cold water makes the blood circulate better."

"Sure," I muttered through chattering teeth. I hurried back to the room and compared notes with Milli, who had just been worked over by a Valkyrie version of Siegfried.

After two full days of a water diet—water and nothing but water—I was called by the doctor and told I could eat anything I liked, although he would determine the amounts.

It was a return to life. I mentally readied my order. Plates of Tsarina risotto with salmon and vodka, *capricciosa* pizzas, Palermo's famed *pasta con le sarde* (pasta with sardines, pine nuts, wild fennel and toasted breadcrumbs). But I realized that I couldn't appear so greedy, and so I said with false nonchalance, "I'll just have some pasta with peas."

"Of course!" smiled the doctor.

After he left, I chastised myself. What on earth had made me ask for pasta with peas, something I would never order in a restaurant and wouldn't have been served at home? Yet that night I quieted the rumblings of my stomach by concentrating on the vision of a steaming plate of pasta, brimming with peas and butter and plenty of good parmesan cheese.

The clinic's dining room opened at 12 o'clock sharp. By 11:00 I was in front of the closed glass doors. By 11:40 there was a long line of ravenous patients waiting to get in. When the doors finally opened, I rushed in and sat down. At last the meal I had been dreaming of for hours appeared: a few strings of spaghetti with five peas.

On day five, lounging listlessly in the sunshine, waiting to go eat half a carrot and an olive, Milli suddenly asked me: "Luca, how much is being starved costing us?"

I told her. She looked at me in amazement.

"For heaven's sake, we can starve at home... for free!"

We left immediately.

| | |

When you are in the middle of a situation such as our fight against the Mafia for a long period, you often fail to see how small, incremental changes have added up. It is similar to looking at your face in the mirror over the years: you assume that the image you see there is pretty much the same as it always was, but then an old friend sees you and blurts out, "Good God, what happened to you?"

In early 1995 I got a sudden insight into how much life in Sicily had changed when I heard from my press aide, Andrea Scrosati, that the American television personality Geraldo Rivera wanted to come to Palermo and do a special report on the Mafia. He wanted me and my administration to help.

Rivera arrived on schedule and began familiarizing himself with the city. I greeted him, but after that I concentrated on my work. Then I began getting reports from my aides that he wanted bodyguards. Why does he need them? I asked. They said they didn't know, but he was insisting. At this point, Italian hospitality took over and I gave him some bodyguards. Then, a day or so later, one of them came to me to tattle: "Now Geraldo has gotten himself a bulletproof vest."

We investigated further and discovered that Rivera planned to set up his film crew in the middle of a downtown square and, after introducing his show, dramatically stand back and pull off his jacket to reveal the bulletproof vest as a testament to how dangerous it was to be in Palermo.

I didn't begrudge Geraldo his foolish pretence about being in danger. But all of this frivolous theatricality made me realize how much our civic life had changed in the last few years, and how absurd posing in a bulletproof vest in the middle of Palermo now was. That was yesterday's news. We were now a society of law and order in a way even I sometimes failed to appreciate, a society where murder was becoming the rarity it should be, rather than a daily occurrence. This was the hot story of Palermo, the story a real investigative journalist should have been desperate to capture. For all those years we were the only region of Italy reported on almost daily by the world's media. And we had been known for one thing: the Mafia. But something had happened. Now that old reality which we had created and exported (and which had come back to haunt us in images created by Francis Ford Coppola and others) was no longer valid. The world had something else altogether to learn from Palermo, and it had to do with civic rebirth, not bulletproof vests.

I considered trying to get Rivera to do this story—the real story of Palermo in the mid-1990s. It had so many fascinating aspects, after all. For instance, the way we had broken the loyalties between Mafia bosses and the soldiers on whom they depended, beginning in the central institution of the jail.

Over the years, Cosa Nostra had perfected a whole parody of social security when one of its own went to prison—taking care of the soldier's kids through monthly handouts, making sure the wives remained faithful to their husbands, handling all aspects of the family's social business. We began to break this system by locating city services in our prisons. We wanted to allow these low-level soldiers a place where they could get the certificates involving property taxes and other matters without having to depend on a Cosa Nostra network. We set up centers where they could play with their children. We gave the wives work helping to arrange public events for the city so they wouldn't have to depend on the monthly Mafia check. We did all this because we knew that for every person in jail there were ten or so people on the outside depending on him. If he stayed in the Mafia orbit, they did too. If he broke away, maybe they would follow.

We encouraged these prisoners to find honest work after they served their time, and we put particular emphasis on forming cooperatives to take on public contracts. One of the first and largest was called Pretoria Bellini. Comprising dozens of former prisoners, this cooperative cleaned monuments such as the Spasimo, a place where antimafia meetings now took place. When Palermo decided to have a large open-air concert in memory of Falcone and Borsellino, at the very spot where Totò Riina was captured, the Pretoria Bellini helped with the preparations.

This was the real story, with the sort of symbolism I believed would make good television. But my press aide advised me that Rivera wouldn't be interested. "Better just to pull the plug on him," Andrea said. So we withdrew cooperation with his show, and Geraldo took his bulletproof vest and went home.

| | |

On September 26, 1995, Palermo was once again full of journalists from all over the world. As ten years earlier, they had come to report on a trial. There were not hundreds of defendants this time, as in the Maxitrial, but only one: Giulio Andreotti. Palermo's prosecutors, now headed by a man named Giancarlo Caselli, had formally indicted Andreotti for being connected with the Mafia. A tenuous accusation had first been made in 1993; two years later, the charge was amplified to "direct involvement" in the Mafia.

Now at the end of his long career, Andreotti, called "the Fox" by those who admired him and "Beelzebub" by those who didn't, had been made a senator for life. He had purposefully made himself into a symbol of Italy in the postwar era. And now it was a country's historical experience that was on trial.

The case against him summoned up all the bizarre complexities of Italian politics over the last quarter-century. Prominently mentioned at the trial was banker Michael Sindona, who used his Vatican connections to build a vast empire of banks on both sides of the Atlantic and was credited by Andreotti in the early 1970s with being "the savior of the lira." Then his empire crashed and he was indicted for fraudulent banking in a scheme that could have destabilized the Bank of Italy. Sindona fled to the United States, where, after being indicted by American authorities for bribery, fraud, embezzlement and corruption—and having at least one meeting with Andreotti—he faked his own kidnapping in 1979 and fled to Sicily. There he lived under the protection of the Mafia before moving on to other European countries and finally returning to New York as a guest of the Gambino family. Sindona was eventually brought to trial in Italy and sentenced to a maximum security prison, where he died after drinking a cup of poisoned coffee.

The prosecutors presented a complex narrative that was the legal equivalent of a page-turning novel. They claimed that Andreotti's point of contact in Sicily had always been Salvo Lima, who had raised the Sicilian share of the Christian Democrats' vote from 2 to 10 percent. And they charged that he had met with Lima and Vito Ciancimino in Rome in the mid-seventies to solidify the relationship, which also involved the Salvo cousins (all of whom referred to Andreotti by the code word "Uncle").

The prosecution tried to show that when the Bontate faction was annihilated in the Second Mafia War, the Corleonesi picked up the relationship with Andreotti through the Salvos and Lima, who, despite their connections to the losing side, were allowed to live because of their value as go-betweens. This new relationship was strained by the Maxitrial and the legal appeals that followed.

Supposedly, there had been a meeting to smooth things out at the home of Ignazio Salvo. Lima was present and so was Totò Riina, who kissed Andreotti on both cheeks in greeting. But the Corleonesi had become disaffected at the time of the Supreme Court appeal, when their old CD allies were no longer able to help them.

The prosecutors called over four hundred witnesses. The case against Andreotti relied heavily on the testimony of *pentiti*. (There were now dozens of them!) Francesco Mannoia told of Andreotti and the Bontate faction. Leonardo Messina described the relationship with Lima, Ciancimino and the Salvos; and Baldassare Di Maggio, a former Riina henchman, told of the kiss.

Most interestingly, Tommaso Buscetta came to testify from his haven in the U.S. Witness Protection Program. While telling everything he knew about the Mafia's military operations, he had previously always stopped short of describing the political connections, saying that it was a story so incredible that if he told what he knew about it, all his other revelations would not be believed. When Andreotti's defense attorneys claimed that Buscetta was now fabricating testimony he had never before mentioned, the prosecution called U.S. federal attorney Richard Martin to the stand. Martin had done much of the debriefing of Buscetta in the United States and had used his information to make the Pizza Connection case. He now testified that when he asked Buscetta in the mid-1980s to reveal what he knew about the Mafia's political assets, Buscetta kept replying that he couldn't, there were profound reasons why he couldn't talk about this subject. Martin had pressed him to say what they were and finally Buscetta had replied with one word: "Andreotti."

One part of the prosecution's case involved the photography of Letizia Battaglia, who had taken thousands of shots of Palermo official functions over the years. In going through her archives, investigators found shots of Andreotti with the Salvo cousins, whom he claimed never to have met. Andreotti dismissed them as random shots taken at functions where he didn't know many of the people with whom he was brought together.

For four years, the Andreotti trial would function as Italy's ongoing soap opera. Then in October 1999, after over four years of legal wrangling, the verdict came in. Andreotti was not guilty on the basis of a particular article of the law, emphasized by the judge as he read the verdict, which focuses on "insufficient evidence."

While confirming Andreotti's close political and personal relationship with Salvo Lima, who, wrote the judges, "both before and after his involvement with the Andreottiani faction, [had] established a permanent collaboration with Cosa Nostra" and had "transformed the Andreottiani faction in Sicily into a structure at the service of the Mafia," the verdict stated that the prosecution had not proved that Andreotti himself "had specific dealings which could be considered as having criminal relevance." Andreotti's relations with Vito Ciancimino, wrote the court, showed a certain "indifference" on his part with regard to Ciancimino's "notorious" links to the Mafia, but on the other hand this "did not unequivocally mean an illegal association."

The verdict was appealed by the prosecutor's office, permissible under the Italian system. The case will be re-examined by a superior court. History will be the final judge.

| | |

One of my favorite quotations is from the great Czech novelist Milan Kundera: "The triumph of man over power is the triumph of memory over forgetting." The importance of keeping memory alive is not just so the past will not repeat itself, or even so the past will continue to provide lessons.

Today in Sicily, a villa once owned by a great Mafia drug lord is now used as a therapeutic community for recuperating drug addicts.

Thirty-nine homeless families were recently assigned to apartments once owned by Vito Ciancimino.

In another Mafioso's villa, a group of nuns administers a home for unmarried mothers, all of them cast out by their families.

A large agricultural property in Ciaculli, once owned by a branch of the Greco family, now belongs to Palermo and is used for agricultural experimentation.

These are just a few of the confiscations. We make sure to publicize each of them—one of our ways of triumphing over forgetting.

Another way is to use our historical experience to help in the fight against organized crime in other countries. How much a symbol Palermo has become in this struggle was clear in December 2000, when over a thousand delegates from 143 countries and more than six hundred journalists gathered in Palermo for the signing conference of the United Nations Convention Against Transnational Organized Crime.

This treaty was designed to assist in the fight against the international Mafias in their various guises, a fight that the United Nations now realizes must be one of the major international law enforcement efforts of the twenty-first century. The treaty pulls down the walls of banking secrecy, criminalizes Mafia-type associations, simplifies extradition and international examination of witnesses, strengthens efforts to eliminate traffic in drugs and human beings, and makes international money laundering more difficult and costly for organized crime.

The signing was a solemn occasion, rich in historical significance for those of us who had lived in Sicily in the second half of the twentieth century. The conference lasted four days, during which the delegates, using the Palermo experience as a starting point, talked about how educators and civic groups, the media and the church, working side by side with law enforcement, can change societies caught in the suffocating grip of criminality and corruption. That entire mid-December week, during which an international antimafia began to form in the middle of our city, was marked by spectacularly sunny, unseasonably mild weather. I am by nature a rational man, but I was tempted to think that Someone Up There had made us this gift so that Palermo, long a dark and bloody place, could now be seen by the rest of the world shining in all its splendor.

| | |

Throughout its long history, Sicily has never had military heroes. We have no statues to warriors. For us, heroism has always been tied to social conscience. We honor *carabinieri* or soldiers who sacrificed their lives during the Second World War to save innocent people from being executed by the Nazis. More recently we have the stirring examples of policemen and women, of magistrates and politicians who gave their lives to rid the country of a plague almost as bad as fascism.

The Mafia's attempt to make us believe that it was composed of "honorable" soldiers who defended true Sicilian values was a tragic farce. If we, once looked down upon as a despicable people who allowed ourselves to be enslaved, can escape from this plague, so too can Russia and all the other countries that find themselves in the grasp of criminality.

There are those who rightly regard the fight against communism as the great battle of the twentieth century. Now that communism has fallen, the new front line to save freedom and democracy is the battle against international criminality. Particularly in some countries recently freed from communism, the Mafia has taken its place in controlling people's lives. If this is allowed to stand, the people might say, as some Sicilians did during our fight: "We were better off when we were worse off." This is an outcome that cannot be tolerated, for it will demoralize the world.

No less than other tyrannies, the Mafia destroys liberty, mortifies democracy, makes economic development impossible and kills the very concept of citizenship. Yet as we here in Palermo know, when such tyrannies are finally broken, the human spirit blossoms.

Acknowledgments

This book is a chapter of my life, and also a chapter of the history of Sicily at the turn of the millennium.

What is more, it gives me an opportunity to ask the forgiveness of Milli, loving companion ever since her days of roller skates and pigtails, and Eleonora and Leila, our daughters, who had to live their own sweet and now distant years of roller skates and pigtails without their father.

I robbed the three of you of the time that was your due, in order to prevent many others from robbing millions of Sicilians of their dreams and rights.

A word of thanks to Davide, son-in-law become son, who with Eleonora made me a happy grandfather. Also to Andrea Scrosati, who was willing to be close to me in both the sunny and the stormy days of my life; to Enzo Lo Dato, who succeeded in combining the will for change with respect for the rules; and to Cecilia Todeschini, friend and comrade in the battle for rebirth ever since the beginning.

And finally, to my parents, Salvatore and Eleonora, and to my grandson, Paolo, with the love of a son and a grandfather: the pledge that I shall keep on being myself.

Index